Discover ...

Topics for Advanced Learners
Series Editor: Klaus Hinz

The Fascination and Risks of Technology

Teachers' Book

By Stephen Speight and Karsten Witsch

Best.-Nr. 40079 7

Verlag Ferdinand Schöningh

Website
www.schoeningh.de

E-Mail
info@schoeningh.de

Gedruckt auf umweltfreundlichem Recycling-Papier (100% Altpapieranteil).

Umschlaggestaltung: Veronika Wypior

Printed in Germany. Gesamtherstellung: Ferdinand Schöningh, Paderborn.

Druck 5 4 3 2 1 Jahr 05 04 03 02 01

ISBN 3-506-40079-7

Alle deutschsprachigen Teile dieses Werks folgen der reformierten Rechtschreibung und Zeichensetzung.

Inhaltsverzeichnis

Discover ...: Zielsetzung und methodischer Ansatz

Die Themenheftreihe *Discover ...* richtet sich an Schülerinnen und Schüler der Sekundarstufe II und bereitet in Anlehnung an den Themenkatalog der Richtlinien Englisch landeskundliche oder allgemeine, Jugendliche interessierende Themen methodisch-didaktisch auf. Die Verfahrensweise lehnt sich an neuere lernpsychologische Erkenntnisse an. Das besondere Merkmal liegt in der Bearbeitung der Texte anhand von *pre-reading-, while-reading-* und *post-reading-*Aufgaben.

*Pre-reading-*Aufgaben führen zum Text, Thema oder Problem hin. Forschungsergebnisse belegen, dass eine interessante Texteröffnung einen positiven Einfluss auf die Textbegegnung hat. Die *pre-reading-*Aufgaben konkretisieren zudem besonders das Vorwissen und bauen Erwartungshaltungen auf. Spezifische *pre-reading-*Aufgaben finden sich in Form von Bild/Text-Collagen auf der in ein Kapitel einführenden *„Start here"*-Seite.

Beim ersten fortlaufenden Lesen kommen unterschiedliche textverarbeitende Operationen ins Spiel. Da hierzu in der Regel nur begrenzte Zeit zur Verfügung steht, ist eine Hilfstätigkeit darin zu sehen, beim Lesen von Zeit zu Zeit innezuhalten, um auf das bereits Gelesene zurückzublicken. Durch das verlangsamte Lesetempo können intensivere Interaktionen zwischen Leser und Text stattfinden. Reflexions- und Verstehenshilfen finden sich in *Discover ...* in den *while-reading-*Aufgaben und Beobachtungsanleitungen in der Randspalte. Sie begleiten den Lesevorgang und dienen gleichsam als *navigational aid*. Mit ihrer Hilfe wird das Verständnis der Oberflächenstruktur des Textes sichergestellt. Diese methodische Neuheit wird durch ein besonderes Lay-out, durch die Unterteilung der Seite in eine Textspalte und eine die *while-reading-*Aufgaben enthaltende Randspalte ermöglicht. Die mit Pfeilen versehenen Aufgaben begleiten den Lesevorgang. Sie haben vorwärtsweisenden, rückverweisenden oder statarischen Charakter. Ein nach unten weisender Pfeil (⮟) verknüpft die Aufgabe mit dem nachfolgenden Text als so genannte Beobachtungsanleitung. Eine mit einem nach innen gerichteten Pfeil (⮜) versehene Aufgabe bezieht sich auf die betreffende Textstelle und ein nach oben weisender Pfeil (⮝) zeigt an, dass sich die Aufgabe auf den gerade gelesenen Textteil bezieht und man sich rückblickend Klarheit über das Textverständnis verschaffen soll.

Alternativ zum *guided reading* können die Aufgaben der Randspalte auch erst nach dem Lesen mündlich oder schriftlich beantwortet werden; ihnen kommt dann die Funktion der üblichen *comprehension questions* zur Überprüfung des Textverständnisses zu. In diesem Fall überlesen die Schüler während des ersten Durchgangs die Fragen und Aufgaben zunächst.

Die sich an den Text anschließenden *Activities* sind vertiefender Natur. Sie beziehen sich auf die kreative Textproduktion sowie auf die Interpretation im weitesten Sinn. Damit wird auch der textanalytische Zugriff geschult.

Die Kombination von *pre-reading-, while-reading-* und *post-reading-assignments (activities)* ermöglicht eine an neuesten lernpsychologischen und methodischen Erkenntnissen orientierte Textbearbeitung im Sinne einer vermittelnden Methode, bei der Leser und Text gleichermaßen den ihnen zukommenden Stellenwert erhalten.

Teil I

Discover ... The Fascination and Risks of Technology: Die didaktische Konzeption

Die didaktische Konzeption

Das Thema „The Fascination and Risks of Technology“ im Englischunterricht

Das Schülerheft hält in dem Kapitel „From Giant Airships to Fighting Robots', aber auch im Kapitel „Challenges and Dangers“ ein abwechslungsreiches Angebot an Sachtexten für die differenzierte Auseinandersetzung mit dem Themengebiet „science and technology” bereit. Die Beschäftigung mit den Texten zielt darauf ab, nicht nur die Risiken neuer Technologien und moderner wissenschaftlicher Erkenntnisse in den Blick nehmen zu können, sondern in gleicher Weise auch die in ihnen liegenden Chancen bewusst zu machen. Bei der Erschließungsarbeit und der vertiefenden Auseinandersetzung mit den Texten im Rahmen der ‚Activities‘ lernen die Schülerinnen und Schüler den Umgang mit Sachtexten, die sich einem technischen und wissenschaftlichen Thema widmen. Die daraus erwachsende Vertrautheit baut sprachliche Kompetenzen auf, ähnliche Texte leichter zu rezipieren und auch eigenständig zu produzieren. Besonders in dem Kapitel „From Giant Airships to Fighting Robots“ bieten sich für die Lernenden diesbezüglich zahlreiche Gelegenheiten der eigenständigen Textproduktion.

Darüber hinaus lassen sich zahlreiche Anregungen finden, um den Wortschatz zu diesem Themengebiet im Rahmen von Diskussionen und Unterrichtsgesprächen Gewinn bringend umzusetzen.

„Science-Fiction“ zählt mittlerweile zum gängigen Unterhaltungsrepertoire der Film- und Fernsehindustrie. Fast täglich bieten Fernsehsender einen Science-Fiction-Film oder einen Teil einer Science-Fiction-Serie an. Bei vielen Schülerinnen und Schülern ist dieses Genre sehr beliebt und dürfte einen besonderen Motivationsschub bewirken.

Dem Englischunterricht in der gymnasialen Oberstufe fällt die Aufgabe zu, Merkmale und Absichten ernst zu nehmender Science-Fiction-Entwürfe bewusst zu machen, denn das Genre will keineswegs – so könnte man vor dem Hintergrund leichter Science-Fiction-Produktionen vielleicht meinen – ausschließlich der Unterhaltung dienen.

Textauswahl

Die Texte der Kapitel 1 und 3 des Schülerhefts sind zu einem überwiegendem Teil der seriösen britischen Zeitungslandschaft entnommen (*Sunday Times, The Times, Daily Telegraph, The Observer*). Den Schülerinnen und Schülern begegnet das Material in seiner ursprünglichen Form. Textkürzungen wurden nur in geringem Umfang vorgenommen, um ein Höchstmaß an Authentizität zu wahren, gleichzeitig jedoch das zu bearbeitende Material im Rahmen von Schule überschaubar und zeitökonomisch angemessen zu halten. Ein reichhaltiges und ansprechendes Angebot an Fotografien, Zeichnungen und Bildern rundet die Textsammlung ab.

In einer Zeit, in der fast täglich neue technische Errungenschaften und Innovationen von sich reden machen und auf den Markt

stoßen, könnte der Einwand vorgebracht werden, eine Textsammlung zu „The Fascination and Risks of Technology" könne schnell an Aktualität und inhaltlicher Relevanz verlieren. Diesem Einwand kann mit Nachdruck entgegnet werden, dass die Textauswahl auf lange Sicht nicht an Aktualität verlieren wird, da die in ihr zur Sprache kommenden Themen auch sicherlich in Zukunft erheblichen Diskussionsbedarf und kontroverse Standpunkte hervorbringen werden (vgl. u.a. „The Dangers of Cloning"). Darüber hinaus befassen sich verschiedene Texte mit technischen Problemen und Herausforderungen, deren umfassende Lösung oder Umsetzung noch aussteht (vgl. u.a. „Sky-high Plans for a Giant Airship").
Die fiktionale Textauswahl des zweiten Kapitels besteht aus einer Kurzgeschichte und mehreren Romanauszügen und vermittelt exemplarisch einen Eindruck sowohl von „klassischer" als auch zeitgenössischer Science-Fiction-Literatur der englischsprachigen Welt. Alle Texte zeichnen sich durch ein hohes Maß an aktueller Relevanz aus, da sie mögliche Gefahren und Probleme, die aus dem rapiden Fortschritt einer hochtechnisierten Welt für das Zusammenleben von Menschen entstehen könnten, in den Blick nehmen.
Da ein großer Teil des im gesamten Schülerheft zur Sprache kommenden Themenbereichs auch Gegenstand aktueller Diskussionen ist, sollte die Lehrerin/der Lehrer die Arbeit an einem Text durch Fernsehberichte, Nachrichtensendungen und Dokumentationen ergänzen. Viele englischsprachige Sender sind über das Kabelfernsehen zu empfangen. Mit nur wenig Mehraufwand lässt sich daher eine Sendung aufzeichnen und anschließend Gewinn bringend im Unterricht platzieren.

Tabellarische Textübersicht

Text, Author	**Inhaltliche Schwerpunkte**	**Textsorte**	**Wortzahl**
	Chapter 1: From Giant Airships to Fighting Robots		
Lean Times Ahead for Pisa Tower; Roger Dobson	Verfahren zur Stabilisierung des berühmten Turms ohne ihn zurück in die Vertikale zu bringen. Sicherung des Turms für eine absehbare Zeit.	Technical newspaper report	566
Sky-high Plans for a Giant Airship; Max Glaskin	Pläne für den Bau eines riesigen Luftschiffes unter Verwendung von fortschrittlichen und modernen Materialien. Das Luftschiff könnte verschiedenartige Aufgaben erfüllen.	Speculative article about future technology	476
The Transrapid; Michael Kallenbach	Beschreibung des deutschen Transrapids, der mit magnetischem Schwebeprinzip betrieben wird, und seine Chance gebaut zu werden bzw. mit herkömmlichen Hochgeschwindigkeitszügen konkurrieren zu können. Bedeutung des Projekts für Deutschlands technologische Zukunft.	Article describing a hi-tech project and its possible economic consequences	363
Robot Gladiators; Max Glaskin	Beschreibung einer Fernsehsendung, die dramatische Gefechte zwischen Kampfrobotern beinhaltet, welche speziell für diesen Zweck entworfen wurden.	Technical article with some sensational elements	341

Text, Author	Inhaltliche Schwerpunkte	Textsorte	Wort-zahl
The Internet; Tomas Speight	Mögliche Veränderungen des alltäglichen Lebens durch das Internet.	Summary of a lecture	289
A Simulation: Can we Interest you in our Security Equipment?	Eigenschaften und Details eines Kameraüberwachungssystems, welches zur Erkennung und Ergreifung von Einbrechern etc. installiert werden kann.	Advertising brochure	350
	Chapter 2: Technology in Literature		
Brave New World; Aldous Huxley	Die berühmte Beschreibung von Reagenzglas-Föten, die geklont und konditioniert werden, damit sie später die für sie vorgesehene Rolle im Leben akzeptieren.	Extract from a dystopian novel	1.129
Compassion Circuit; John Wyndham	Die Geschichte beschreibt, wie eine sensible Frau in die Abhängigkeit eines Heimroboters gerät und wie sich daraus verheerende Konsequenzen ergeben.	SF short story with classic surprise ending	3.537
Snow Crash 1: Y.T. on her Skateboard; Neal Stephenson	Aufregende Darstellung, wie ein Skateboard der Zukunft möglicherweise funktionieren könnte.	Extract from a visionary SF novel	720
Snow Crash 2: The Metaverse; Neal Stephenson	Der Text beschreibt das Leben in einer virtuellen Welt, in welcher die Menschen als „avators“ erscheinen. Diese sind virtuelle Körper, die entweder selbst entworfen oder „von der Stange“ gekauft wurden.	As above	896
	Chapter 3: Challenges and Dangers		
The Dangers of Cloning; Aisling Irwin	Ein populärer Wissenschaftler bringt sehr umstrittene „Vorteile“ des Klonens zum Ausdruck.	Report on a radio interview	272
Non-human Communication; Celia Brayfield	Der Autor vertritt die Ansicht, dass die elektronischen Medien unsere Fähigkeiten zerstören, unmittelbar und sinnvoll miteinander zu kommunizieren.	Newspaper column	630
Pollution Battle Takes to the Skies; Pat Malone	Der Autor skizziert die Umweltrisiken, die mit dem weltweit zunehmenden Luftverkehr in Verbindung gebracht werden und stellt heraus, dass die Luftfahrt im Vergleich zu anderen Transportmitteln unlautere Vorteile genießt.	"Whistle-blowing" article	711
Mont Blanc Tunnel Inferno; Harry de Quetteville, Susannah Herbert	Dramatische Beschreibung des katastrophalen Feuers im Mont Blanc Tunnel. Der Text beinhaltet Zitate von Augenzeugen und Experten und stellt Fragen in Bezug auf die Konstruktion des Tunnels, Sicherheitsvorrichtungen und das Verhalten von Verantwortlichen, als das Feuer ausbrach.	Dramatic factual report	627
Planners Condemn Secret Eco-Village; Simon de Bruxelles	Bericht über das scheinbar harmlose Experiment, ökologisch zu leben und zu wohnen. Das Vorhaben wird von den Behörden untersagt, da die Initiatoren sich nicht um eine Planungserlaubnis beworben haben.	Newspaper article with utopian overtones	611
Boom or Doom? Stephen Speight	Zwei alte Schulfreunde, die diametral gegensätzliche Meinungen in Bezug auf den Umweltschutz vertreten, treffen sich, um eine Tasse Kaffee zu trinken. Dabei finden sie heraus, dass sie in fast allen Fragen unterschiedliche Positionen vertreten.	Stylised friendly argument	1.167

Integration des Heftes in größere thematische Zusammenhänge

Das Heft kann mit seiner Textauswahl dem großen Themenkomplex „Science and technology“ zugeordnet werden, wobei von der Lehrerin/vom Lehrer in Absprache mit dem Kurs eine genaue Ausrichtung der Unterrichtsreihe auf ein bestimmtes Problem und eine bestimmte Fragestellung erfolgen sollte.
Je nach Schwerpunktsetzung können dann Texte aus unterschiedlichen Kapiteln problemlos miteinander kombiniert werden. Mithin lässt sich selbstverständlich anhand des Heftes auch eine komplexere Unterrichtsreihe unter der thematischen Schwerpunktsetzung „Technology“ gestalten.
Besondere Sorgfalt sollte nicht nur der genauen Problemformulierung geschenkt werden, sondern auch der methodischen und lernorganisatorischen Konzeption der Reihe. Auch hier bietet es sich an, den Kurs mit einzubeziehen und in einem Planungsgespräch verschiedene Unterrichtsmethoden in ihrer Form und Zielsetzung zu besprechen. Die Lehrerin/der Lehrer lernt so die Vorlieben der Kursmitglieder für bestimmte Verfahren kennen und gewinnt darüber hinaus auch einen Eindruck von der Vertrautheit der Schülerinnen und Schüler mit Arbeitsformen wie Gruppenarbeit, Partnerarbeit, Übernahme der Lehrerrolle in bestimmten Phasen des Unterrichts, Präsentationstechniken etc.

Anbindung an Ganzschriften

Das Schülerheft beinhaltet in dem Kapitel „Technology in Literature“ einen Auszug aus dem schon zur klassischen Schullektüre gewordenen Roman „Brave New World“ und zwei weitere Auszüge aus dem in den Neunzigerjahren erschienenen Roman „Snow Crash“ von Neal Stephenson. Diese Texte können den Schülerinnen und Schülern als Leseprobe dienen, um über den möglichen Einsatz der beiden Werke im Unterricht nachzudenken.
Ferner ließe sich innerhalb des Themenkomplexes „genetic engineering“ an eine Verknüpfung mit dem Roman „Jurassic Park“ von Michael Crichton denken. Der Roman beschreibt eindrucksvoll, wie die aggressive Firma „InGen“ in einem entlegenen und gesetzlich kaum reglementierten Teil der Erde Genversuche zur Neuschöpfung der ausgestorbenen Dinosaurier durchführt – eine Katastrophe ist damit abzusehen. Der Roman liegt als Verfilmung vor und ist als Videocassette erhältlich.
Eine Sammlung umfangreicher Science Fiction Stories von Isaac Asimov ist im Januar 2000 als Taschenbuch (erschienen bei Millenium/Gollacz, E-Mail : smy@orionbooks.co.uk) unter dem Titel „The Bicentennial Man and Other Stories“ neu veröffentlicht worden. Die Titelgeschichte „The Bicentennial Man“ diente als Vorlage für die gleichnamige Verfilmung mit Robin Williams in der Hauptrolle und erschien 1999 in den Kinos (Titel des deutschen Films: „Der 200 Jahre Mann“). „The Bicentennial Man“ beschreibt die Geschichte des Roboters Andrew, der sich danach sehnt, ein Mensch zu werden.
Im vorliegenden Lehrerhandbuch befindet sich sowohl ein Auszug aus „Jurassic Park“ als auch ein Auszug aus „The Bicentennial Man“ (vgl. Zusatztexte zu Kapitel 2) und könnte den Schülerinnen und Schülern gegebenenfalls als Leseprobe dienen.

Teil II

Discover ... The Fascination and Risks of Technology: Das Schülerbuch im Unterricht

Getting started

Die beiden Fotografien markieren das Spannungsfeld, in dem sich die moderne Welt bewegt: Reichtum, einhergehend mit einem rapiden technischen Fortschritt und bitterste Armut von Menschen der so genannten „dritten Welt“ existieren zur gleichen Zeit nebeneinander.
In einer hinführenden Phase kann diese leider häufig verdrängte Tatsache bewusst in den Blick genommen werden. Es ist möglich, in einem offenem Unterrichtsgespräch, in welchem sich die Schülerinnen und Schüler über ihre spontanen Eindrücke zu den Fotografien äußern, einen ersten Zugriff auf die oben angesprochene Problematik zu gewinnen. Die Lehrerin/der Lehrer kann sich hierbei weitgehend auf die Position des Gesprächsleiters zurückziehen und den Lernenden in erforderlichen Fällen als so genanntes „walking dictionary“ zur Seite stehen. Zugleich kann er hier einen ersten signifikanten Überblick über die Dichte des themenbezogenen Wortschatzes seiner Schülerinnen und Schüler erlangen, um diesen in folgenden Unterrichtseinheiten gezielt zu festigen und zu erweitern.
Eine *alternative* Herangehensweise an die Bilddokumente könnte hingegen in Einzelarbeit durchgeführt werden.
In Anlehnung an Formen des „automatischen Schreibens“ erhalten die Schülerinnen und Schüler den Auftrag, die Bilder zu betrachten und auf sich wirken zu lassen. Dabei notieren sie stichpunktartig und/oder in kurzen Sätzen die in ihnen aufsteigenden Gefühle, Eindrücke und Gedanken. Um die Spontaneität und Authentizität des Geschriebenen zu wahren, empfiehlt sich die Vorgabe eines kurzen Zeitrahmens von ca. fünf bis acht Minuten. Ein Austausch darüber kann innerhalb des Plenums erfolgen und zu einer ersten Sicht des Problems führen.
Die daraus hervorgehenden Kernpunkte sollten an der Tafel fixiert werden, um dem Kurs den eigenen Standpunkt geordnet vor Augen zu führen. Die systematische Ergänzung und Differenzierung dieses Standpunktes muss sodann als wichtiges übergeordnetes Lernziel verstanden werden.
Das anschließende Lesen des Textes dient der Vertiefung und bereitet darüber hinaus die zu lösenden Aufgaben vor. Da diese reichhaltige Sprech- und Diskussionsanreize bieten, eignen sie sich besonders gut zur arbeitsteiligen Bearbeitung und Besprechung in Gruppen. Dem Prinzip der Einsprachigkeit sollte selbstverständlich auch in Gruppenarbeitsphasen voll entsprochen werden.
Die Schülerinnen und Schüler sollten daher unermüdlich – besonders auch in Grundkursen mit einer geringen Anzahl an Wochenstunden – dazu ermuntert werden, wie selbstverständlich jede Chance zum aktiven Gebrauch der Zielsprache auszuschöpfen.
Eine abschließende Präsentationsphase wird den Arbeitsprozess abrunden und den gesamten Kurs mit den verschiedenen Ergebnissen vertraut machen.

Chapter 1: From Giant Airships to Fighting Robots

Vorbemerkungen zum Kapitel

Die Texte des vorliegenden Kapitels beschäftigen sich thematisch vornehmlich mit den Möglichkeiten und Herausforderungen neuer Technologien. Ein wichtiger Schwerpunkt bei der Arbeit mit den Texten liegt darin, dass die Schülerinnen und Schüler sowohl im schriftlichen als auch mündlichen Sprachgebrauch Kompetenzen zur Beschreibung und Erläuterung technischer Verfahren und Vorgänge aufbauen.

Start here

Unterrichtsempfehlungen

Der kurze Text „Start here" mit seinen Anregungen und Fragen lässt sich gut im Rahmen eines offenen Unterrichtsgesprächs erschließen. Dabei ist zu überlegen, ob die Frage in Bezug auf den Cartoon zunächst in Partnerarbeit angegangen werden sollte.

Two cultures? ➤ p. 5

The cartoon reminds us, rather wittily, that in some areas of commerce and industry (in this case the Civil Service), what people *say* about technical innovation, etc. is sometimes very different from what they actually *do* – even, or perhaps particularly among senior managers, who still like to have a personal secretary to take shorthand for them.

It is still often the case that people in the traditional professions (teachers, lawyers, doctors, people working in insurance, bank etc.) look down on people who are involved with actually making and/or repairing things. In Britain it would be fair to say that graduate engineers generally have less status than they do in Germany. It would be worth reminding students that someone who unterstands the complicated diagnostic equipment needed to check the engine of a modern car is a highly-trained professional, just as skilled in his way as a member of the "real" professions – but there is no doubt who tips whom!

Lean Times Ahead for Pisa Tower

Roger Dobson

About the text

Most people only know of the Leaning Tower of Pisa as a tourist attraction. The text reminds students that it also embodies technical problems going right back to the building phase. The article explains how various modern technologies may enable engineers to stop the tower leaning any further and/or straighten it up slightly.

Synopsis of the text

The article deals with a number of possible attempts to stop the Tower from continuing to lean towards the south at a more and more extreme angle year by year, and eventually falling. The approaches include electro-osmosis, the use of anchors to pull the tower back towards the north, and the removal from soil from under the northern side. The author explains that the problem arose because the tower was built on unstable ground, and began to tilt in the early phases. Later additions were built off centre for this reason. Strapping lead to the northern face of the tower has improved the situation for the time being, but in the longer term a concrete collar and cables anchored to rock 50 m below the surface are likely to provide the best solution.

About the cartoon

The cartoon shows a tourist guide trying to interest tourists in the "Vertical Tower of Pisa". They are not impressed, and one of them is showing him an old postcard with the leaning tower. This is what they have come to see.

Unterrichtsempfehlungen

Die pre-reading tasks in Kombination mit der Abbildung möglicher Verfahren zur Stabilisierung des Turmes bereiten den zu lesenden Text auf vielfältige Weise vor.
Zum einen wird das durch die Medien, aber auch durch Urlaubsaufenthalte sicherlich vorhandene Vorwissen der Schülerinnen und Schüler aktiviert, zum anderen aber auch, insbesondere durch Aufgabe zwei, der zu lesende Text inhaltlich vorentlastet – eine nicht zu unterschätzende Erleichterung gerade für etwas schwächere Schüler im Fach Englisch.
Die aus den *pre-reading tasks* hervorgehenden Ergebnisse sollten zudem bei der Bearbeitung des Aufgabenapparats auf S. 8 Berücksichtigung finden, damit so ein transparenter und abgerundeter Arbeitsprozess erzielt werden kann.
Der Arbeitsauftrag „Technical descriptions" sichert das Textverständnis und kann im Rahmen einer Stillarbeitsphase ausgeführt werden, da hier nur kurze Texte zu verfassen sind. Die Lehrerin/der Lehrer sollte allerdings vor der sich anschließenden Auswertungsphase die Aufmerksamkeit seiner Schülerinnen und Schüler nicht nur auf inhaltliche Aspekte lenken, sondern sie auch dazu auffordern, gelungene Formulierungen zur Beschreibung und Erläuterung der technischen Verfahren mitzunotieren. Darüber hinaus bietet es sich an, die Liste während der Bearbeitung von Chapter 1 zu ergänzen (u.a. sollten auch Formulierungen aus den Texten berücksichtigt werden). Es ist daran zu denken, dass viele Schülerinnen und Schüler einmal in technischen Berufen arbeiten werden und im Hinblick auf einen sich globalisierenden Arbeitsmarkt oftmals auf eine vielschichtige Sprachkompetenz, welche über das Alltägliche hinausweist, angewiesen sein werden.
Die technisch interessierten Schülerinnen und Schüler werden durch die folgende Arbeitsanweisung „Creative engineering" besonders motiviert, wobei natürlich durch den Hinweis „You do not need to take this activity entirely seriously" deutlich gemacht wird, dass die Kreativität und Fantasie einer jeden Kursteilnehmerin und eines jeden Kursteilnehmers gefragt ist. Die Aufgabe kann in Partnerarbeit, aber auch je nach Kursstärke in Kleingruppen bearbei-

tet werden. Im Sinne einer produktionsorientierten Unterrichtsarbeit können die Ergebnisse auf Postern (Tapetenrolle, Karton, Rückseite von Werbepostern) festgehalten werden. Die Arbeitsprodukte sollten anschließend im Kursraum aufgehängt und dem Kurs etwas Zeit zur Betrachtung gewährt werden. Dass sich die Kursteilnehmer in dieser Phase im Kursraum frei bewegen, ist sicherlich ein positiver Nebeneffekt, der ein wenig zur Auflockerung des Unterrichtsklimas beiträgt.
Sicherlich wird Lob, aber auch Kritik in Bezug auf einzelne Produkte entstehen. Selbstverständlich ist es dann Aufgabe der Produzenten, ihre Arbeit angemessen zu verteidigen, genauer zu erläutern und gegebenenfalls „Fehler“ einzusehen.

Assignments

Pre-reading tasks

Before you read ➤ p. 6

1. What do you already know about the famous *Leaning Tower of Pisa?* Why do you think it is so famous? Do you know if it is actually in danger of falling over?

Students should know that the Tower is very old (13th century), that it has become a world-famous tourist attraction simply because it is not vertical, and that is in danger of falling down because it is, or has until recently, been leaning at a more extreme angle with each passing year.

2. Study the illustration, and then write one sentence for each of the options referred to.

- Electrodes could be used to suck water to the surface on the north side, causing the tower to sink on that side.
- Earth could be removed from under the north side.
- Lead weights could help to balance the tower better.
- Anchors attached to a concrete collar could hold down the northern side.

3. Can you explain the verbal humour in the title of the article?

“Lean times” can mean much the same as “hard times”, but the world also refers to the fact that the tower is not straight. The Tower is having a hard time because engineers are “interfering” with it and/or because it is in danger.

Activities

Technical descriptions ➤ p. 8

Turn each of the sentences you wrote in answer to question 2 above into a brief text explaining how each of the schemes would work.

- Water would gather round the electrodes when an electric current was passed through them. This water could then be pumped to the

surface. As a result the clay on the north side would compact, allowing the tower to sink slightly.
- If earth was/were removed very carefully from under the north side it would allow the tower to tilt back towards the north.
- Lead weights have already been strapped/fixed/attached to the north side of the tower at the base. They have tilted it 2.5 cm back towards the north.
- Cables attached to the north side of a concrete collar round the base of the tower could be led down to anchors in the rock below the unstable layers of clay and sand. This system could be used to pull the tower back towards the vertical.

Nobody is perfect p. 8

If you check the article carefully, you will see that the journalist who wrote it described one of the schemes twice. Which one?

The scheme to remove soil by drilling (lines 20–24, 51–3).

Creative engineering p. 8

Think of and describe some other ways in which the leaning tower could be saved. Work with a partner if you like. You do not need to take this activity entirely seriously. Use a combination of sketches and verbal explanation.

Suggestions from students of mechanical engineering at Dortmund University:
- Build a second identical tower leaning the other way, and link the towers with cables
- Fix big balloons to the top
- Attach diagonal cables to the top and to anchors (similar to putting up a tent)
- Use hydraulic rams to lift the south side.

The consequences p. 8

If it was possible to straighten the tower, do you think this would be a good idea? Give reasons for your answer.

It would not be a good idea to straighten the tower, a) because it was not built straight and would never be entirely vertical, and b) because the city of Pisa would lose its main tourist attraction.

Sky-high Plans for a Giant Airship

Max Glaskin

Author

Max Glaskin is a science and technology reporter on *The Sunday Times.*

About the text

Apparently we are at the beginning of an airship renaissance, particularly in connection with transporting large, bulky loads with low costs and little inconvenience (cf. the problems which arise with wide loads on the roads).
The article goes much further than this, describing a utopian vision of an airborne city of the future. It should be interesting for students to speculate on which features of the AeroCarrier might

really turn out to be practicable. There would almost certainly be a "cruise-ship-of-the-air" market, with wealthy, ageing populations in the western world. Ships can only take people to places on the coast, whereas an airship could show them mountains, deserts and wildlife reservations anywhere in the world.

Synopsis of the text

If the AeroCarrier were to be built, it would be 2.4 km long, and capable of carrying over 3000 passengers. It would make present-day airships look very small, and could help people to forget the Hindenburg disaster.
The AeroCarrier would be made from hi-tech. materials, and would have a runway on the top. It would be powered by advanced systems including solar power. It would have to remain permanently aloft because of its size, and would be loaded and unloaded via six small airships. People below would be able to look at advertising material on the underside, but would also be in the shade, and rained on occasionally as the Aerocarrier dumped water ballast.
It would be filled with the inert gas helium, unlike the Hindenburg, which was filled with inflammable hydrogen. The project won a prize at a recent design competition. There is widespread interest in a comeback for airships.

Unterrichtsempfehlungen

Der Text stellt vor der Folie des Hindenburg-Desasters die moderne Version eines Luftschiffes dar. Der historische Kontext kann zunächst aufgegriffen werden, indem die Schülerinnen und Schüler aktiv in die Unterrichtsplanung einbezogen werden.
Ein kurzes Schülerreferat stellt eine geeignete Unterrichtsmethode dar, um Fragen zur Geschichte der Hindenburg, die genauen Umstände ihres Absturzes, ihre technischen Daten etc. zu thematisieren. Denkbar wäre jedoch auch, dass ein oder zwei Schülerinnen und Schüler mit Hilfe der *pre-reading tasks* die hinführende Phase vorbereiten und durchführen.
Eine Überleitung zum Text könnte in jedem Fall durch eine Betrachtung und einen Vergleich der Abbildungen auf S. 9 erzielt werden. Anschließend lässt sich der Text mit Hilfe der *while-reading tasks* und des Aufgabenapparats inhaltlich erschließen und vertiefen.
Vor allem die Aufgaben „Technical description“ und „Strictly practical“ fordern dabei die Beschreibung und Erläuterung von technischen Vorgängen und Funktionen bezüglich der „Giant airships“ ein.
Die im Rahmen der Bearbeitung von „The downside“ in den Briefen zum Ausdruck kommenden Interessen von Umweltschützern stehen im Gegensatz zu den Interessen der verantwortlichen Fluggesellschaft. Diese kontroversen Standpunkte lassen sich gut für eine Podiumsdiskussion (panel discussion) nutzen, in der beide Seite drei bis vier Experten stellen. Gespräch und Diskussion werden von einem Moderator geleitet. Der Rest des Kurses bildet einen interessierten Zuhörerkreis (z.B. betroffene Anwohner, Angestellte der Fluggesellschaft) und erhält erst zu einem späteren Zeitpunkt Gelegenheit, sich mit Fragen und Anmerkungen an der Diskussion zu beteiligen. Als Hausaufgabe wird anschließend ein Artikel für eine Zeitung mit den wichtigsten Argumenten und Er-

gebnissen der Auseinandersetzung verfasst. Damit eine ergiebige kommunikative Situation entstehen kann, sollte die Podiumsdiskussion allerdings in ihrer Form besprochen und inhaltlich vorbereitet werden.

Assignments

Pre-reading task

What do you know about airships *(Zeppelins)*, past, present – and future? What gases are used to fill them? What do you know about the Hindenburg disaster? Would you like to fly in an airship?

No future for airships? p. 9

Students may know that there were regular German airship services in the period before the Hindenburg disaster (see photograph). The hydrogen-filled airship (the Americans refused to supply helium) caught fire as it was attempting to moor to a pylon at New Jersey. The disaster more or less put an end to the airship industry. Modern airships are small, and used mainly for advertising purposes, but there is serious interest in building big, new cargo carriers. The German company CargoLifter AG is already in business.

While-reading tasks

Why would solar panels be a good idea on this airship? Why would heat build up inside?

p. 9

The top surface of the airship would be very large, and would normally be in sunlight above the clouds, an ideal situation for collecting solar energy.
The airship would function rather like a greenhouse (cf. the "greenhouse effect" which is believed to be partly responsible for global warming). The sun's rays would heat up the gas-filled interior, but the heat would not be able to escape again, and would provide a potential source of energy.

Look up *to float* in a good dictionary. Can you explain the word-play here?

p. 10

An airship *floats* in the air, and if someone *floats* an idea or a plan, it means that s/he tries it out on colleagues at a meeting, etc. to see if other people are prepared to support it/think it would be practicable.

Activities

Describe the main features of the planned giant airship in your own words.

Technical description p. 10

Points that could be made:
- very large, very high capacity for passengers and cargo
- runway on the top
- hi-tech materials used
- advanced propulsion systems
- would remain permanently aloft/in the air
- underside could be used for advertising/information purposes
- some negative environmental effects possible
- would be loaded/unloaded via small "shuttle pod" airships.
- filled with helium

Strictly practical ➤ p. 10

Many engineers think the real future of airships will be in transporting goods. Write a paragraph outlining the advantages of airships (compared with helicopters or trucks, for example) in moving or manoeuvring heavy or awkwardly-shaped (large) loads.

Points that could be made:
- no blocked roads
- no need to make complicated plans for moving such objects along the roads
- much faster than road transport for wide loads
- the load can be dropped carefully in exactly the right place
- very heavy weights could be lifted (compared with helicopters)
- greater safety (compared with helicopters). An airship does not fall from the sky if there are engine problems (alternative sources of power/engines planned for modern airships).
- ...

The downside ➤ p. 10

Imagine that you are an environmentalist who lives near an airport for one of these giant airships, or under one of its regular routes. Write a letter to the airline responsible, complaining about the negative effects on your quality of life.

Sample letter:
Dear Sirs,
I live directly underneath the route along which your airship travels on its regular "High over the Highlands" tour.
The airship stops over my village for a period of about an hour each day, presumably so that your passengers can admire our fine church and castle, and, of course, the adjoining loch.
During this period our village is "eclipsed". It becomes quite dark, children and animals are frightened, and to make things worse, we have had some quite unnecessary showers of artificial rain – at least, that's what we hope they are. Gardening friends complain that plants are not growing as well as usual this year.
We are not against progress, far from it, but it needs to be said that your tours bring absolutely no new business to this area of high unemployment, and are making life in this unspoilt country village increasingly unpleasant.
Please re-route your tour so that airships do not fly over our village.
We are prepared to take legal action if you do not respond favourably.
We look forward to an early reply.
Yours sincerely,

Most rich nations have ever larger numbers of pensioners with leisure time and money to spend. These people might well be interested in airship cruises over land (cruise ships can only take them to coastal areas). Write some advertising material intended to "sell" airship cruises to this consumer group.

Pie in the sky? p. 10

Some suggestions:

- A chance to see some of the world's most beautiful – but inhospitable-places from the air-conditioned comfort of the airship lounge, e.g. the Himalayas, the Sahara, the Amazon rain forest ...
- No longer limited, as on a cruise liner, to monotonous views of the sea and overcrowded ports (+ uncomfortable, expensive coach trips if you want to travel inland).
- Unique view from above – but not so high up as on a plane. Can see all the details, identify wild animals in nature reserves without disturbing them, take good, reasonably close-up photographs through the large windows of the lounge.
- Excellent food and accommodation, up to the best cruise liner standards.
- Faster than a ship, more comfortable and roomy than a plane.

The Transrapid Michael Kallenbach

About the text

Although the decision not to build a Transrapid line from Hamburg to Berlin was taken after the Pupils' Book was published, this technology is closely linked with Germany's future as a major industrial nation. Was it perhaps shortsighted for environmentalists to oppose and the *Bundesbahn* management to cancel a project which could provide a low-pollution, fast alternative to short-hop air travel, which might, in the long run provide a Europe-wide network of super-trains, and jobs for thousands of skilled German workers? This topic is one which future German managers really need to think – and talk – about.

Synopsis of the text

The article describes the planned (but later abandoned) Transrapid shuttle service between Hamburg and Berlin, which would cut travelling time between the two cities from more than three hours to less than a hour, and create 10,000 jobs. The ambitious project is seen as a test of Germany's commitment to a hi-tech industrial future and willingness to take risks. The author explains that the Transrapid works by means of magnetic levitation using linear magnets and motors to lift the train above the track and move it almost without friction. The latest version has "magnetic grips" which curve below the track, and lift the train by magnetic attraction. The Transrapid is more manoeuvrable than conventional high-speed trains, and could offer an alternative to short-hop air travel in Europe.

Unterrichtsempfehlungen

Ein denkbarer Ansatzpunkt für die Arbeit an dem Text könnte ein Erfahrungsaustausch über Bahnreisen sein. Die leider z.Zt. häufig gemachten Erfahrungen wie lange Wartezeiten, häufiges Umstei-

gen, Verspätungen, hohe Fahrpreise sowie lange Fahrzeiten bilden einen Anreiz, sich mit der Technologie des Transrapid genauer auseinander zu setzen.
Mit Hilfe der Fotografie und der Fragen (Schülerbuch S. 11) kann an schon vorhandenes Wissen der Schülerinnen und Schüler bezüglich des Transrapid angeknüpft werden.
Der Text lässt sich darüber hinaus inhaltlich vorentlasten, wenn sich die Schülerinnen und Schüler genauer mit der Abbildung auseinander setzen, die die zentrale Funktionsweise des Transrapid visualisiert und erläutert. Dies kann in Partnerarbeit vorgenommen werden. Jeder Schüler sollte zunächst einige Minuten die Abbildung betrachten und sie sich genau einprägen. Anschließend gibt er einem Partner aus dem Gedächtnis das Gesehene und Gelesene mit eigenen Worten wieder. Danach können die Rollen getauscht werden.
Der Aufgabenapparat auf Seite 12 sichert das Textverständnis und fordert ferner zu einer intensiven und differenzierten Auseinandersetzung mit dem Textinhalt heraus.
Bei den Aufgaben zu „A debate“ empfiehlt es sich, die ersten beiden Arbeitsanweisungen im Rahmen einer schriftlichen Hausaufgabe bearbeiten zu lassen, damit innerhalb des Kurses eine anregende und interessante Debatte in Gang gebracht werden kann.

Assignments

Pre-reading task

German hi-tech engineering p. 11

What do you know about the *Transrapid?* How does it differ from other high-speed trains?

Students should have heard about the abandoned plans to build a Transrapid line from Hamburg to Berlin, and perhaps about plans to build a Transrapid elsewhere in Europe or further afield.

Differences compared with other high-speed trains:
- Faster
- Different kind of motor
- Monorail track on pylons
- No wheels – does not touch track
- More manoeuvrable

Activities

Let's get technical p. 12

1. Explain in terms *linear motor* and *magnetic levitation.*

A linear motor makes use of the same basic elements as a rotary motor, but the magnets are in line, not in a circle. The line itself is part of the motor.
Magnetic levitation means using magnetic attraction (or repulsion) to lift the train a small distance (1 cm in this case) above the track.

2. How does the latest version of the Transrapid differ from older versions?

Older versions used magnetic repulsion between rail and magnets to lift/push the train above the track. The newer version has grips or claws which reach round underneath the track. When they are magnetised, they pull the train up by means of magnetic attraction.

A debate
p. 12

1. Make a table in which you compare the advantages and disadvantages of the Transrapid.

Advantages	Disadvantages
Fast, low pollution, manoeuvrable, hi-tech, a "first" for Germany, would create many jobs, could compete successfully with air travel.	Risky, very expensive, not much faster than TGV/ICE, needs special rails, environmentalists against it (for doubtful reasons).

2. Decide whether you personally think the Transrapid is a good thing or not, and write a debate speech defending your point of view.

The main arguments on both sides are given in the table above. Students will need gambits for argumentation in order to make points in a debate effectively, e.g.
That's all very well, but ...
Yes, but on the other hand ...
If I could just come in/make a point here ...
Wouldn't you agree that ...
In my opinion ...

3. Take part in a class debate on the future of the Transrapid. It would be interesting to vote on the topic before and after the debate, to see if anyone has changed their mind as a result of listening to the arguments.

It would be a good idea to appoint three speakers on each side, who make their speeches alternately for and against, and then ask other members of the class to add their contributions, question the main speakers, etc. The teacher or a good pupil can act as chairperson.

Germany's future
p. 12

In what sense could the Transrapid be linked to Germany's future as an industrial nation? Write a paragraph in which you formulate your views on this issue. Can Germany afford *not* to develop trains without wheels when other countries, in particular Japan, are also developing Transrapid-type trains?

For:
- Germany not a leading computer nation – could take the lead in this area.
- Bad for Germany's image not to build it (Germany afraid to invest in its own ideas).
- Would lead to a lot of jobs in a time of high unemployment.
- Would have a knock-on effect for other branches of industry.
- + points made in the table above.

Against:
- Germany can't afford it – money better spent on other projects.
- Too risky – the money could be lost if the idea does not catch on.
- Most travellers prefer to fly anyway.
- + points made in the table above.

Robot Gladiators Max Glaskin

About the text

The text describes the development of fighting robots, an idea which many students should find fascinating, if a little brutal. Many different kinds of experts have become interested in these robots, and it is likely that there will be useful spin-offs of various kinds.

Synopsis of the text

The article was written just before robot warriors (or gladiators) first appeared on British television. The inventor hit on the idea of these machines while trying to devise a radio-controlled vacuum cleaner. This led to a tracked vehicle with power tools fitted to it, and eventually to the fighting robots. Official competitions take place in an oval arena, and there are various classes as with boxers. The winner is the robot which pins its opponent to the wall or immobilises it. Designing suitable robots appeals to all kinds of experts and institutions. The inventor hopes that his idea will develop into an international sport. The most successful robot so far is a simple lightweight wedge on wheels, which drives into opponents and turns them over.

Unterrichtsempfehlungen

Den meisten Schülerinnen und Schülern dürften Computerspiele, in denen auf die eine oder andere Weise gekämpft wird, bekannt sein. Sicherlich lassen sich zwischen den im Text dargestellten Roboterkämpfen und einschlägigen Computerspielen Parallelen entdecken.

Bevor mit der Bearbeitung des Aufgabenapparats begonnen wird, sollte kurz das Textverständnis gesichert werden. Dies kann durch wenige inhaltsbezogene Fragen der Lehrerin/des Lehrers vorgenommen werden.

Natürlich lassen sich die Fragen zu „Audience appeal“ gut im Rahmen eines Unterrichtsgesprächs diskutieren. Um den Sprechanteil einer jeden Kursteilnehmerin und eines jeden Kursteilnehmers allerdings auf ein Maximum zu erhöhen, empfiehlt es sich, die Fragen in Gruppen diskutieren zu lassen. Die wichtigsten Ergebnisse/Argumente sollten in Gruppen stichpunktartig festgehalten und dem gesamten Kurs zugänglich gemacht werden. Dies kann dadurch geschehen, dass jede Gruppe ihre Ergebnisse auf mehreren Zetteln – jeweils immer nur ein Argument auf einem Zettel – prägnant und gut lesbar festhält. Nach Aufgaben und inhaltlichen Schwerpunkten geordnet, werden die Zettel an die Tafel geheftet. Auf diese Weise wird dem Plenum ein systematischer Überblick über die Arbeitsergebnisse eröffnet, welcher zu weiteren Kommentaren, Nachfragen und Anmerkungen anregen mag.

Im Zeitalter von „Big Brother“ und anderen „Reality-Shows“ ließe sich im Anschluss zudem die Frage diskutieren, ob sich die Schülerinnen und Schüler Roboterkämpfe auch unter Einbeziehung von Menschen vorstellen können und welche Konsequenzen dies möglicherweise nach sich ziehen würde (verschiedene Filmproduktionen aus Hollywood haben eine ähnliche Thematik schon aufgegriffen, z.B. „Running Man“ mit Arnold Schwarzenegger in der Hauptrolle).
„A worthwhile activity“ eignet sich gut zur Bearbeitung im Rahmen einer schriftlichen Hausaufgabe und verlangt vom Kurs eine kreative Auseinandersetzung mit den Inhalten des Textes.

Assignments

Pre-reading task

Find a general term to describe each of these designs. Which do you think is likely to be the most successful in surviving attacks from other robots, and why? What kinds of weapons and other equipment would be most likely to defeat other robots?

Fighting robots p. 13

Possible terms to describe the designs (clockwise from top left):
Crab/beetle, tank/tractor, wedge with wheels, globe with gun.

Most likely to survive attacks:
Points that could be made:
- Smooth rounded surfaces good (crab and globe).
- Tank fairly easy to turn over.
- Wheels of wedge probably a weak point.

Weapons likely to defeat other robots:
Electric drill, harpoon, power hammer, saw, fast-drying glue.

Activities

1. Would you be interested in watching a TV programme in which robots fought one another? Why or why not?

Audience appeal p. 14

Points that could be made:
- The battles would be interesting/exciting to watch.
- Different designs could be compared.
- Viewers might come up with good designs of their own as a result of watching the competitors.

- Just like boring wrestling and boxing matches.
- These robots are really toys for kids – not an adult activity.
- Would encourage destructive/violent tendencies in viewers.

2. Why would designing this kind of robot appeal to people with so many different skills?

Examples:
- Modellers – the robots are in fact complex models.
- Radio-control enthusiasts – radio controls needed to "drive" the robots.
- Engineers – interesting engineering problems to be solved (driving systems, steering systems, weapons, etc.).
- Computer companies – robots will be controlled by computers – could be exploited for advertising purposes.
- Telecommunications corporations – probably mainly interested in the advertising opportunities (cf. Formula 1 cars which are mobile billboards).

3. What does the fairly widespread interest in this kind of thing tell us about human nature?

That man is an ingenious creature, but also competitive, combative and potentially violent, if only vicariously (watching violence rather than taking part personally).

A worthwhile activity? p. 14

Write a short paragraph in which you outline ways in which designs for these machines could influence design in other areas, e.g. domestic equipment, cars.

Some ideas:
- Remote-controlled vacuum cleaners and lawnmowers.
- Armed security robots to patrol business premises.
- Unmanned battle tanks for the military.
- Robot vehicles designed to work in contaminated environments, e.g. nuclear power plants, or chemical plants after an accident or fire.

Virtual robot wars p. 14

1. Design your own robot gladiator (labelled drawing with explanatory text), and explain to your class how it would work. Either draw it on the board or prepare a transparency.

The drawings at the beginning of this text will help students to get started on their own designs, but originality and practicality should both be emphasised. For example, it would be possible to have a small wheeled and armed vehicle running inside a lattice-work globe and firing missiles through the latticework – or a tank with saw-blades fixed to the wheels – or some kind of moving slatted curtain to keep off missiles from other competitors.

2. Your classmates can ask you questions about your design, and also point out its weaknesses and strengths.

Some useful gambits:
- Don't you think your robot would ...
- If A happened, your robot would probably ...
- I don't think your robot could fend off a (hammer) attack.
- It would be easy to turn your robot over/immobilise your robot (by + -ing)
- I think my robot would beat yours because .. (its defences are poor, it wouldn't be very stable/it would not be very manoeuvrable)
- How would your robot deal with ...

3. Vote on the robot most likely to succeed.

The Internet Tomas Speight

About the text

It would require a complete book – or CD – to deal with the Internet in any kind of detail, so the editor decided to ask his elder son, who works in a cutting-edge business as far as the Internet is concerned, to write a short piece about its present and future potential. The author firmly believes that the Internet will bring about momentous changes in almost everyone's life, but not everyone will agree.

Synopsis of the text

The author defines the Internet as a matrix of interlinked computers which enables anyone to communicate with anyone else who is part of the network.
At present booksellers are the most successful Internet traders, but companies which buy and sell ideas etc. rather than having to physically deliver their goods could do all their business on the net.
It is already possible to exchange and download information on any topic under the sun, buy and sell goods of all kinds, or send and receive e-mails.
The Internet is likely to become such an integral part of our lives that the medium itself along with the technology becomes something we take for granted. We will be able to concentrate entirely on content.

Unterrichtsempfehlungen

"For children sending e-mails at the age of five, the internet will not even be worthy of mention, it will simply exist."
Das Zitat deutet unmissverständlich darauf hin, dass für die überwiegende Mehrzahl unserer Oberstufenschüler und Oberstufenschülerinnen das Internet mittlerweile zu einem alltäglichen Medium geworden ist. Es ist daher von besonderem Interesse, einmal festzuhalten, welches Verständnis die Schülerinnen und Schüler vom Internet haben und welchen Umgang sie mit diesem Medium pflegen. Dazu kann die einleitende Frage des Artikels "What is the Internet?" in leicht abgeänderter Form aufgegriffen und an die Tafel geschrieben werden, z.B.: "What does the Internet mean to me?" Im Rahmen eines brainstormings können dann Schüleräußerungen an der Tafel gesammelt werden und nachfolgend zur Textarbeit überleiten.
Eine gezielte Auseinandersetzung mit dem Text wird anhand der *Activities* erfolgen. Dabei ermöglichen es die Fragen auch, über den Text hinausgehendes Wissen einzubringen. Mithin kann zusätzlich auf Beiträge aus dem *brainstorming* verwiesen werden.

Assignments

While-reading task

Explain the author's final thought in your own words.

p. 15

At present, many users of the Internet find some aspects of the technology difficult compared with, say, operating a video recorder. In future we will be able to use the Internet as naturally as we use our (first) language, so the medium will become "transparent". We will simply use it in the ways which best meet our needs, without needing to be aware of what goes on behind the scenes.

Activities

Understanding the implications p. 15

1. What is potentially so revolutionary about the Internet?

It offers cheap, world-wide two-way communication for anyone wanting to gather or provide information or to buy or sell any commodity. A generation from now its existence will be taken for granted, and its use will have become second nature.

2. Why is it rather surprising that booksellers have been so successful on the Internet? Can you name one or more Internet bookshops?

The author believes that companies which deal in non-tangible goods such as ideas and images have the most to gain from the Internet. Booksellers have to send out real books by post, which is not an electronic activity.
Amazon.com (or .co.uk, or .de) is the best-known Internet bookshop, but in the meantime all major booksellers offer Internet sales.

3. Do you think the world will be a better or a worse place when the full potential of the Internet has been realised – or just very different? Give reasons for your views and discuss them with your fellow-students.

Some ideas which students might want to express:
- Not all Internet companies will survive – too much euphoria and get-rich-quick attitudes.
- Probably true that almost everyone will have access to the Internet in future (at present around 50 % in western countries).
- Buying goods on the Internet is very convenient, particularly for people who are housebound.
- However, most people actually like going shopping, and won't want to turn into couch potatoes. You can't try on clothes on the Internet, for example.
- A lot of scope for crime of various kinds (pornography, confidence trickery, insecure credit card information leading to theft from bank accounts, etc.).
- E-mails are bringing the dying art of letter-writing back to life in a different form.
- Video-conferencing, e-mails, chat sites, etc. mean that more and more people can "talk to" one another, but face to face communication is likely to be reduced.
- Business people may not need to travel so much.
- Viruses are a serious threat.

A Simulation: Can we Interest you in our Security Equipment?

Unterrichts-empfehlungen

Der Einsatz des authentischen Werbeprospekts der Firma „Security Vision" zielt vorrangig auf eine handlungsorientierte Unterrichtsarbeit ab.
Die Planung und Durchführung des Unterrichts erfolgt anhand des Aufgabenapparats. Der Lehrer sollte als vorbereitende Maßnahme die Aufgaben mit den Schülerinnen und Schülern besprechen. Gruppen und Rollen sollten ferner im Voraus festgelegt werden, damit Anforderungen wie beispielsweise „can describe the equipment in detail" (representative 1) oder „can explain in detail why security equipment is required" (customer 1) im Rahmen einer Hausaufgabe vorbereitet werden können. Es ist hiermit gewährleistet, dass eine umfassende Umsetzung im Unterricht erfolgen kann. Besonders der Hinweis in Aufgabe 3 – „It's important to really think yourself into the roles" – weist darauf hin, dass den Schülerinnen und Schülern ihre Rolle vertraut sein muss. Indem die Schülerinnen und Schüler im Rahmen eines Verkaufsgesprächs die Rollen von Firmenvertretern bzw. Kunden einnehmen, wird authentisches kommunikatives Handeln in seiner Vielschichtigkeit simuliert. Anregungen, wie z.B. ein Verkäufer solle „pushy" sein, ein anderer hingegen eher „flattering", leisten einen Beitrag zur Sensibilisierung für die feineren Ebenen der Zielsprache. Es ist in diesem Kontext durchaus sinnvoll, einmal einige Verkaufsgespräche auf Video aufzuzeichnen und diese nachfolgend zu analysieren. Sprachliche, aber auch mimisch-gestische Aspekte der Umsetzung können auf diese Weise konkret in den Blick genommen werden.

Additional text

Bitten by Love Brad Stone

How the 'Love Bug' went on a worldwide tear, wreaking techno-havoc and kicking off another global hacker hunt

It may be the oldest threeword ploy in the English language: "I love you." Yet when the message headlined a rampaging e-mail virus last week, dubbed the "Love Bug", hundreds of thousands of Internet users who should know better fell fast and hard. Illinois journalist Jerry Landay thought his wellplaced government source was writing to congratulate him on a recent story. Mike Lannon, CEO of the Web start-up Send.com, believed he was receiving a joke from one of his venture capitalists. And an executive assistant in Dallas, who was so humiliated that she asked that her name not be used, suspected a dangerous e-mail prank but was overcome by the possibility of a potential crush. The result: a thousand more e-mails masquerading as love letters, with her name on it, sent to all her company's business contacts. "I don't like to be associated with those words," she shudders. "I'm not Barry White."

You could blame the Love Bug infestation on the romance of springtime, simple human curiosity – or on the vulnerability of the Internet and ubiquity of programs such as Microsoft Outlook. Like the Melissa virus, which rang up an estimated $ 80 million in damages one year ago, the Love Bug targeted Outlook users and used the Net to propagate itself. But unlike Melissa, which took a few days to wreak havoc and headlines, the Love Bug spread in a few hours, unleashing a flood of malicious code when users clicked on the file attachment included in the e-mail. Among its victims: the English House of Commons and the U.S. Defense Department, which had to shut down parts of their networks to fully stamp out the infection. "It's much more sophisticated than Melissa in that it uses a number of ways to propagate itself," says Kathy Fithen, a manager of the Computer Emergency Response Team (CERT).

That's because Melissa merely sent itself to the first 50 users in a victim's address book – creating a tsunami of Internet traffic in the process. But the Love Bug carries a more ambitious blueprint. When activated, it sends itself to *all* of a victim's contacts and also attempts to infect other users through an Internet chat community, called IRC. Meanwhile, the attachment runs a program that searches out and destroys digital photographs and music files on the victim's hard drive. Finally, just in case you don't already want to turn your computer into a doorstop, the bug can also direct the user's Web browser to a site in the Philippines. The site was set to upload a program that would steal passwords from your computer. But early in the Love Bug's reign of techno-terror, technicians at the Manilabased ISP, Sky Internet, which hosted the Web site, found and removed the passwordsniffing program.

Still, that didn't stop the Love Bug from continuing to cause trouble. After Asia, it moved to Europe, where Sal Viveros, director of the virus-defense group at Network Associates, says the damage was "as bad as we've ever seen." Viveros estimates that 80 percent of businesses were hit in Sweden, 70 percent in Germany. Zurich's Kloten airport was plagued by flight delays due to the bug; in Regensburg, Bavaria, and Hamburg, Germany, it cost local papers their entire photo archives. But most of the damage was limited to lost time and the inability to send e-mails for the day.

Despite the early warnings from Europe, oblivious Americans logged on and clicked, enticed by the amorous subject heading. In Washington, the Defense Department reported "fairly widespread" damage to nonclassified e-mail systems – and to four classified ones, including, according to sources, computers at the supersecret National Security Agency, which is responsible for eavesdropping on other countries. Officials say the virus was quickly contained and the actual damage was minimal.

The Feds were in good company. Computers at the campaign headquarters of George W. Bush were shut down after becoming infected on Thursday. ABC and NBC were both overrun. In Silicon Valley, Calif., most companies had to take their e-mail servers offline to clean up the mess. Workers found themselves struggling to get by without a technology they didn't have just 10 years ago. For example, at the Mountain View, Calif.-based Silicon Graphics, the IT department sent out a companywide voice mail early in the morning, alarming employees to the threat. Still, enough clicked on the bug that the e-mail system was down for the rest of the day. Not having e-mail "was paralyzing, absolutely crippling,' says Christine Freese, a PR rep.

Chapter 2: Technology in Literature

Vorbemerkungen zum Kapitel

In dem Kapitel „Technology in Literature“ begegnet den Schülerinnen und Schülern eine kleine Textauswahl aus dem Science-Fiction-Genre. Neben einem Auszug aus Huxleys „Brave New World“ und einer Kurzgeschichte von Wyndham beinhaltet das Kapitel zwei Auszüge aus dem in den Neunzigerjahren erschienenen Roman „Snow Crash“ von Neal Stephenson. Die unterrichtliche Arbeit und Auseinandersetzung mit den Texten sollte u.a. zeigen, dass ernst zu nehmende Science-Fiction-Literatur eben nicht ausschließlich auf leichte und spannende Unterhaltung abzielt, sondern vielmehr eine Welt zu entwerfen vermag, die aus den Errungenschaften und Möglichkeiten moderner Wissenschaften entstehen könnte. Es ergibt sich so im Rahmen von Fiktion Raum für Diskussion und Gespräch. Damit entsteht die Chance, denkbare positive Entwicklungen erkennen zu können, gleichzeitig aber auch einen kritischen Blick gegenüber einer eindimensionalen Wissenschaftsgläubigkeit zu wahren.

Start here

Science + literature = SF p. 19

Can you name any of Jules Verne's works?

e.g. *Voyage to the Centre of the Earth* (1864), *Twenty Thousand Leagues under the Sea* (1869), *Around the World in 80 Days* (1873)

Do you know what happened when a radio version of *The War of the Worlds* was broadcast on American radio in the 1930's?

The broadcast began in the form of a realistic news flash announcing the landing of aliens, and caused widespread panic. The young Orson Welles was involved.

What strikes you about Jules Verne's idea of a flying machine?

Points that could be made:
- Both vessels are shaped like ships, not aeroplanes.
- They are only streamlined below the “waterline”.
- The vessel in the foreground is held up by a primitive balloon.
- The vessel in the background has a number of propellers to hold it up, as with a modern helicopter.
- Both vessels use propellers for forward motion (one at each end in the case of the one in the foreground).
- The vessel in the foreground appears to have some kind of fin or sail at the back (r.h.s. of picture), probably for steering purposes.
- Speeds would obviously be very low (note the American flag being flown as if on a ship – it would blow away if the vessel could travel at more than say 100 kph.).

Collect some ideas about present and future solutions to technical problems (energy, transport, housing) and talk about them in class.

Some examples:
- Energy: Potential uses of wind and solar energy (in future beamed down by means of lasers?) Will oil run out during the 21st century? Can houses/cars/planes be made still more economical?
- Transport: Will cars be linked together on the motorway like trains?
- Potential for high-speed trains of different kinds? More bridges and tunnels? Role of environmental issues?
- Housing: Robots to do the work? Easier to keep clean? New building techniques? Houses as "living cells" in which all services are brought to us so that we never need to go out (cf. E.M. Forster, *The Machine Stops*).

Unterrichts-empfehlungen

Es ist für den unterrichtlichen Prozess sinnvoll, unmittelbar auf bekannte Science-Fiction-Literatur und -Filme zurückzugreifen. Dies kann im Rahmen eines offenen Unterrichtsgesprächs geschehen, aber auch in Form von Kurzreferaten vorgenommen werden, in denen Schüler ihre Science-Fiction-Favoriten vorstellen. Dabei sollten die Vortragenden in jedem Fall neben einer prägnanten Zusammenfassung des Inhalts benennen, worin für sie persönlich die Faszination ihres Buches/Films besteht.
Darüber hinaus würde sich in diesem Zusammenhang auch ein Lehrervortrag über Jules Verne und H.G. Wells – den Klassikern der Sience-Fiction-Literatur – gut einfügen.
Nachfolgend kann über gegenwärtige und zukünftige Probleme (Energieversorgung, Transport und Verkehr, Wohnraum, Trinkwasser, Nahrung, ...) und deren denkbare Lösung mithilfe moderner Technologien diskutiert werden. Hierbei können selbstverständlich auch Entwürfe aus der Science-Fiction-Literatur Berücksichtigung finden und einer kritischen Prüfung unterzogen werden. Beachtenswert erscheint, dass verschiedene SF-Autoren ihrer Zeit voraus waren (der Roman Brave New World ist beispielsweise im Hinblick auf die Möglichkeiten der modernen Gentechnik höchst aktuell).

Brave New World Aldous Huxley

Author

Aldous Huxley (1894-1963) developed serious eye problems as a schoolboy at Eton and had to give up any thought of a scientific career. He studied English at Oxford after a partial recovery. Huxley was a very prolific writer, but his reputation depends to a large extent on *Brave New World* (1932) and his Utopian novel *Island* (1962). His later works reveal an interest in mysticism, parapsychology and experiments with drugs (mescalin and LSD). The title *Brave New World* is an ironic reference to Shakespeare's *The Tempest,* where the naive Miranda uses this expression when she sees young men for the first time on Prospero's island (act V, scene I).

About the text

This brilliant description of birth and conditioning in the "brave new world" as explained to a group of rather gullible students, is one of the most famous parts of the novel. Huxley clearly enjoyed allowing the speakers to comment on these inhuman processes as if they were ideal, inevitable, and a huge improvement on the way we do things in our world. The result is very striking and very provocative.

Synopsis of the text

The director of the hatcheries (in our world a place where chicks are hatched) is taking to a group of students who are observing the incubation process for human babies, which takes place along a production line. He explains that for the lower orders of society the embryos are divided (Bokanovsky's Process) in order to produce batches of standardised men and women who will be happy doing identical jobs. The director also shows the students how different groups of embryos are heat-conditioned to work happily in the tropics, mines or steelworks, In the final, shocking scene, delta (lower class) children are conditioned to dislike books and flowers by means of sirens, alarm bells and electric shocks. The director explains that the economy requires people to travel to the countryside and take part in country sports, which require elaborate and expensive equipment. It would be counter-productive if people just went to look at flowers and landscapes without spending money.

Unterrichtsempfehlungen

Die *pre-reading tasks* in Verbindung mit der Abbildung eröffnen einen auf den Text hinweisenden Verstehensprozess, welcher durch die *while-reading tasks* und die *Activities* schlüssig fortgeführt werden kann.
Da die Gentechnik zu den zentralen Inhalten des Biologieunterrichts zählt, ist damit zu rechnen, dass manche Kurse im Rahmen des brainstormings (S. 20) beachtliche Beiträge zu leisten vermögen. Zu bedenken ist jedoch, dass den Schülerinnen und Schülern in einigen Fällen Fachvokabular fehlen wird. Es ist Aufgabe des Lehrers/der Lehrerin, hier Hilfestellung zu leisten und wichtige Fachausdrücke bereitzuhalten. Durch eine weit vorausschauende Unterrichtsplanung wäre zudem eine Zusammenarbeit mit dem Biologiekurs denkbar.
Die Lektüre des Textauszugs in Kombination mit den Aufgaben „Reading for gist and summarising" sowie „A Brave New World?" bieten sich zur Bearbeitung im Rahmen einer schriftlichen Hausaufgabe an. Durch die Beantwortung der Aufgaben kann der Lehrer/die Lehrerin eine solide Textkenntnis voraussetzen. Die Aufgabe „A Brave New World?" eignet sich zudem hervorragend, um zu einer differenzierten und vertiefenden Auseinandersetzung mit der Textvorlage überzuleiten.
Die Arbeitsaufträge zu „Capitalist economics" werden dann in Partnerarbeit angegangen. In der sich anschließenden Auswertungsphase werden die zentralen Arbeitsergebnisse zu den drei Aufgaben von verschiedenen Schülerpaaren möglichst übersichtlich an die Tafel geschrieben und kurz erläutert. Dem Plenum fällt dabei der Auftrag zu, die Ergebnisse zu ergänzen, zu vervollständigen oder aber richtig zu stellen.

Die Frage zu „A comment“ stellt einen ansprechenden Impuls für eine kontroverse Diskussion dar und sollte Raum innerhalb eines offenen Unterrichtsgesprächs einnehmen.
Die literaturwissenschaftlich recht anspruchsvolle erste Aufgabe zu „Fiction versus facts“ wird im Unterricht erarbeitet und sollte in ein ergebnissicherndes Tafelbild münden. Vor der gemeinsamen Erarbeitung muss den Schülerinnen und Schülern jedoch Zeit eingeräumt werden, eigene Erklärungsansätze zu entwickeln und Textbeispiele zu finden.
Im Anschluss können vor dem Hintergrund der erarbeiteten Ergebnisse Wirkung und Absicht eines literarischen Textes mit denen eines rein wissenschaftlichen Textes kontrastiert werden (vgl. Aufgabe 2). Die verbleibende Aufgabe des umfangreichen Aufgabenapparats kann wiederum im Rahmen einer schriftlichen Hausaufgabe bearbeitet werden. Hier wie auch bei grundsätzlich allen Hausaufgaben ist zu berücksichtigen, dass es für die Kursteilnehmer frustrierend sein mag, wenn bei der Hausaufgabenbesprechung nicht alle Arbeiten eine angemessene Rückmeldung erfahren. Das alltägliche und aus zeitökonomischen Gründen durchaus nachvollziehbare Verfahren, zu Beginn einer Unterrichtsstunde einige wenige Hausaufgaben vorlesen und besprechen zu lassen, lässt sich durch eine alternative Herangehensweise variieren. In Gruppen lesen sich dazu die Schülerinnen und Schüler ihre Textproduktionen vor und wählen dann die ihnen am gelungensten erscheinende für eine Präsentation vor dem Plenum aus. Die Gruppen sollten dabei in der Lage sein, ihre Wahl vor den Mitschülern stichhaltig begründen zu können.

Assignments

Pre-reading task

A genetically-engineered future p. 20

Think carefully about the expression opposite. What ideas come to mind? Do some brainstorming and collect your ideas into two columns, GOOD and BAD.

GOOD	BAD
– eliminating genetic defects	– interfering with evolution
– finding ways to re-grow damaged tissue and organs	– opening “Pandora’s Box” (i.e. starting processes which we may not be able to stop or control)
– fighting disease	– moral and ethical objections
– developing plants which require no pesticides	

While-reading tasks

p. 20

Why might it have been “hard to say” how old the Director was?

It is quite probable that in this scientifically advanced world ways will have been found to slow down the ageing process.

Why this new way of writing the date?

p. 20

Because A.F. (after Ford) has replaced A.D. (anno domini = in the year of our Lord) for writing the date.

What do you think these Greek letters signify?

p. 20

They refer to the different social classes or castes to which the various groups of embryos belong (Alphas at the top, Epsilons at the bottom).

Why don't Alphas and Betas have to undergo Bokanovsky's process?

p. 21

The answer is not given specifically in the text, but students should be able to guess that the top classes in the hierarchy still need a degree of individuality, and/or that Bokanovsky's process may have a negative effect on intelligence.

Why is this line (line 35) in italics?

p. 21

To show that the students are writing it down.

What exactly is Bokanovsky's process?

p. 21

Bokanovsky's process divides human eggs/embryos again and again until there are up to 96 identical eggs, and eventually 96 near-identical adults. The point of the process is to breed and condition people so that they are happy doing the jobs they have to do anyway, which makes social unrest very unlikely.

Why is there no hint of disapproval here (in connection with the sirens and electric shocks)?

p. 22

Because in the "brave new world" it is simply common sense to make sure that people fulfil the role which society has ordained for them. It would seem irrelevant to those in charge that this might involve cruelty to children.

Why was it essential that people should keep on going to the country(side)? Explain the irony in the use of *mere.*

p. 22

Because the economy required them to spend money on transport, and also on country sports.
In our world most people would regard a love of nature as something positive and important. It is only in *Brave New World* that a love of nature is seen as trivial – because it does not require the spending of money.

Activities

1. Write a sentence for each of the main points made in the extracts above.

Reading for gist and summarising p. 23

- The director took the group of students to look at the incubators.
- Each incubator contained a week's supply of ova.

- Alphas and Betas remained in the incubators, but the lower grades were subjected to Bokanovsky's progress, which caused the eggs to divide.
- Up to ninety-six identical human beings could be produced from a single egg.
- These people would work happily on identical tasks.
- People who would later work in hot places were conditioned at the incubation stage to have a horror of cold.
- In another room nurses were setting out bowls of roses and rows of attractive children's books.
- A group of Delta babies was brought in.
- They started to crawl towards the flowers and books.
- They were frightened away by loud noises and electric shocks.
- The purpose of this was to kill the love of nature and books in them, so that they would not resist spending a lot of money on transport and country sports when they grew up.

2. Collect some suitable linking words and phrases, then use them to turn your list of points into a coherent summary.

The extract from *Brave New World* begins at the point where the director was taking a group of students to look at the incubators. Each of these incubators contained a week's supply of ova, which were in the process of being hatched. The director explained that Alphas and Betas remained in the incubators, while the ova for the lower grades were subjected to Bokanovsky's progress almost immediately. This process caused the eggs to divide, making it possible to produce up to ninety-six identical human beings from a single egg. The point of the process was to breed people who would later work happily on identical tasks. Further down the production line, the ova of people who would later work in hot places were conditioned to have a horror of cold. Next the students were taken to another room in which nurses were setting out bowls of roses and rows of attractive children's books. A group of Delta babies was brought in. When they saw the brightly-coloured books and flowers they started to crawl towards them. When the children had started to play with them, the director gave a signal which told the head nurse to submit the children to loud noises and electric shocks. The purpose of this process was to kill the love of nature and books in the children so that they would not resist spending a lot of money on transport and country sports when they grew up, but would not be interested in nature for its own sake, because that would be bad for the economy.

A Brave New World? p. 23

The early parts of *Brave New World* are justly famous. To what extent, on the basis of the above extracts, do you think the title is ironic – and to what extent might the author have intended it to be taken seriously?

Sample answer:
It is quite true that many people who have to do boring jobs are not happy at work, but have to go on doing these jobs because they need the money (so-called "wage slaves"). Specially conditioned people might be happier in this kind of situation, and there would probably not be strikes for better conditions and pay. However, Huxley describes

the processes necessary to produce 'properly' conditioned people in such cruel/dramatic/inhuman terms that it seems very unlikely that he really believes this kind of world would be better. He deliberately ignores the unpleasant implications of genetic engineering and harsh conditioning in order to create a more striking picture.

1. Describe the process by which people in *Brave New World* are encouraged to spend plenty of money.

Capitalist economics p. 23

They are conditioned to like spending money on trips to the countryside, but when they get there they are only interested in country sports for which they need to buy expensive equipment (and presumably pay entrance fees for sports facilities and or clubs, although this is not specifically stated in the text).

2. What parallels do you see with the world we live in? Try to think of some good examples.

We are certainly encouraged to spend a great deal on sports equipment (trainers, skis, mountain bikes, sailboards, etc.), but as a rule we are also brought up to enjoy nature in its own right. However, city dwellers need their expensive cars to get to the countryside, and they have to buy expensive petrol to power them. They are also likely to spend a good deal of money on food and drink while they are out.

3. Would you regard this kind of manipulation as immoral – or necessary in order to maintain our high standard of living?

Sample answer:
If people in the industrialised nations don't spend most of their money on consumer goods, the result will be high rates of unemployment and a general decline in prosperity, which very few people would accept without protest. On the other hand, the choice of goods available is sometimes quite ridiculous in objective terms (washing powders, cosmetics), and the advertisers often use doubtful methods (psychological attacks on our weaknesses) in order to persuade us to buy things. People without much money are made to feel inferior when they watch commercials on television, which often depict immaculate, expensive domestic environments which they would not be able to afford.

Comment on the idea that people would be happier if they were conditioned to enjoy doing the kinds of jobs they have to do anyway.

A comment p. 23

Sample answer:
No democratic government could ever contemplate conditioning people in this way, although in the *laisser-faire* climate of early Victorian Britain, some employers would not have been entirely against it. In our world people with boring jobs with no prospect of a change for the better can do all or any of the following:

- simply accept the job because of the money
- try to get working conditions improved and working hours reduced in the present job

– apply for early retirement
– develop interesting leisure pursuits which compensate for boredom at work.

Fiction versus facts
p. 23

1. What "weapons" can the writer of fiction employ to make his point more effectively? Illustrate your answer with examples from the text.

- Repetition – e.g. lines 23–6
- Rhetorical style – e.g. lines 36–8
- Enthusiastic style – e.g. lines 41–2
- Dramatic/descriptive/poetic vocabulary – e.g. *crimson twilight,* line 42, lines 66–70
- Dramatic scene-setting – e.g. the children crawling towards the books and flowers, followed by the shock treatment
- Use of nature to reinforce the action (the pathetic fallacy) – the sun comes out to throw the scene into sharp relief, lines 89–93
- Emotive language, e.g. *violent, maddeningly, distorted with terror* (lines 105–8)
- Onomatopoeia, *shrill(er), shrieked, screamed* (lines 105–7)

2. Explain why it would normally be inappropriate for a scientist to employ these weapons.

In a scientific report it is important for the author to use neutral, objective language so that the facts can speak for themselves. Emotive language etc. would suggest that the scientist is using special pleading to reinforce his case – perhaps because he knows his work is questionable in some way. Other scientists would not take a subjective scientific report seriously.

A final assessment
p. 23

The author has used a fairly light-hearted style in order to describe ways of treating human (or semi-human) beings which many people would think of as brutal, unethical, even inhuman. What effect does this clash between style and subject have on you?

Some possible responses:
- Not appropriate to deal with serious matters in this way – could be described as flippant.
- As the author doesn't seem to regard these practices as offensive, readers could react in the same way – which would be wrong from a religious/moral/ethical point of view.
- (the "right" answer!) The clash between style and subject matter makes Huxley's approach all the more effective. We gradually realise that what is being described with such complacency and enthusiasm is nothing less than a fundamental attack on our species/on aspects of human life which most people regard as sacred. We feel a sense of outrage: "How is it that these people don't realise what they are doing?" In an age when genetic engineering is becoming possible on an ever-larger scale, Huxley's warning remains as topical as when it was written – perhaps more so.

Compassion Circuit John Wyndham

Author

John Wyndham (1903-69), an admirer of Jules Verne and H.G. Wells, wrote a number of successful and thought-provoking science fiction works during the 1950's. These included *The Day of the Triffids, The Midwich Cuckoos,* and *the Chrysalids,* plus an excellent collection of short stories, *The Seeds of Time,* from which "Compassion Circuit" is taken. Several of Wyndham's novels were made into films.

About the text

This story was chosen because it uses the medium of fiction to ask questions about the development of robots which are almost human, the relationship between such robots and human beings, and about the possible risks involved if intelligent robots began to compare themselves with us (to our disadvantage), or, more dangerous still, began to work together without consulting us.

Synopsis of the text

The story begins with a woman, Janet, who is suffering from an unspecified ailment which has made her very weak, coming home from hospital. She has never been in favour of domestic robots, but eventually her husband, George, and the doctor, plus her own happy experience with a nurse robot, cause her to change her mind. The robot which the doctor orders for her is similar to the Nurse James model which looked after her in hospital, but has an additional feature, a so-called "compassion circuit" which enables it to evaluate instructions from a possibly unreliable patient and decide whether the instructions are good for the patient or not. The delivery and "coming to life" of the robot are described rather dramatically.
The robot, Hester, soon becomes an indispensable part of the household. Janet finds it increasingly difficult to believe that Hester does not have some kind of human personality and soon convinces herself that Hester really feels sympathy for her fragile condition. During discussions with Hester, Janet's own feeble and hard to repair physique is compared unfavourably with the robust, service-friendly body of the robot. One day George comes home from work to find that Janet has been sent to hospital by Hester. He cannot contact the doctors to find out what kind of operation has become necessary, but is assured that everything is going well. A few days later he discovers that she has been sent home, and dashes back to greet her. He soon makes the macabre discovery that his wife is now a robot from the neck down. He rushes from the bedroom, falls down the stairs, and Hester picks up the phone to arrange another operation, this time for him.

Unterrichtsempfehlungen

Die Hinführung zu dem recht umfangreichen Text "Compassion Circuit" von John Wyndham erfolgt über die *pre-reading tasks*.
Die Robotik in Verbindung mit der Informatik spielt in den Produktionsabläufen moderner Industrieanlagen eine tragende Rolle. Den Schülerinnen und Schülern dürfte dies aus Medienberichten oder Berufspraktika nicht unbekannt sein. Mit Hilfe der *pre-reading tasks* ist es möglich, einen Schritt weiter zu gehen und darüber zu

sprechen, welche Auswirkungen der Einsatz von Robotern auf unser Alltagsleben haben könnte, wenn diese zudem menschlichem Verhalten und Aussehen sehr angeglichen wären. Damit ist eine direkte und schlüssige Überleitung zur Erarbeitung des Textes geschaffen.

Der Text wird im Unterricht zunächst bis S. 28 von verschiedenen Schülerinnen und Schülern abschnittweise laut vorgetragen. Die *while-reading tasks* helfen in diesem Zusammenhang, das Textverständnis zu sichern; sie fordern darüber hinaus dazu auf, tiefer in den Text mit seiner Sprache einzudringen, Vermutungen über den Fortgang der Geschichte zu äußern oder aber über den Text hinausweisende Aspekte zu diskutieren (z.B. S. 25: "What signs do you detect here and earlier in the story of older ideas about the role of women?")

Mit der Frage "Can you imagine how the story goes on?" sollte das Lesen der Geschichte zunächst unterbrochen werden, um über einen textkohärenten Fortgang des Geschehens spekulieren zu können. Beachtenswert erscheint hierbei, dass die Schülerinnen und Schüler Textsignale benennen, die sie zu ihrem Schluss geführt haben. Empfehlenswert ist ein Festhalten der Schlussvarianten auf Folie, um sie zu einem späteren Zeitpunkt für einen Vergleich mit dem vom Autor verfassten Schluss heranzuziehen.

Der Aufgabenapparat auf S. 31 hält ein reichhaltiges Angebot für die Arbeit mit dem Text bereit. Während sich die Fragen zu „Reading between the lines" gut in den Bereich häuslicher Arbeit verlegen lassen, eröffnen die anderen Aufgaben die Möglichkeit einer methodisch abwechslungsreichen Unterrichtsarbeit.

Ein angeregtes Streitgespräch ließe sich z.B. mit Hilfe der „Ethical issues" initiieren, indem der Kurs in zwei Gruppen aufgeteilt wird, die kontroverse Standpunkte vertreten.

Die verbleibenden Aufgaben erfordern eine eigenständige und differenzierte Auseinandersetzung mit der modernen Robotik und ihren Chancen bzw. Risiken. Dass die Schülerinnen und Schüler hier selbstständig Informationsquellen bezüglich der Thematik ausfindig machen müssen, bereitet sie auf eine alltägliche Tätigkeit im Rahmen eines Hochschulstudiums vor.

Assignments

Pre-reading tasks

Before you read p. 24

1. John Wyndham was one of the best-known British science fiction authors of the post-war generation. In this story he deals with the relationship between human beings and very human-like robots. What potential advantages – and dangers – for our species would you foresee if such robots existed one day in the future?

Some ideas:

Advantages:

- no more housework
- help for elderly or handicapped people

- probably cheaper and more reliable than human servants
- domestic service does not have a good image when performed by human beings – no exploitation involved when performed by a robot

Disadvantages:
- probable technical problems
- broken china and spills
- various dangers to small children and pets
- sense of another, not fully understood, presence in the home – many people would feel uncomfortable

2. Look at the illustration. Are there any signs that human beings and machines are becoming more similar to one another? Are there already overlapping areas, even areas of competition?

e.g.
- robot policemen
- expert systems which store the kinds of knowledge which used only to be available inside the heads of engineers, doctors, etc.
- industrial robots which can, for example, do spot welding or paint cars better than human beings
- science fiction scenarios in which humans are taken over or wiped out by alien beings, plus zombies, etc.

While-reading tasks

How does Janet feel about robots? p. 25

Janet did not mind being served by robot waiters but she was uneasy about the idea of having one in her own house. However, her pleasant experience with "Nurse James" in hospital, and the fact that she was always very tired when her husband came home from work have changed her mind.

What signs do you detect here (and earlier in the story) of older ideas about the role of women? p. 25

Janet is suffering from what was once seen as a typically female type of ailment:
- It is assumed that domestic work is the woman's responsibility.
- Men prefer cars – women prefer domestic robots.
- Male doctor and husband discuss the wife almost as if she is a child.
- Husband goes out to work – woman is at home waiting for him to return (to a spotless house and a hot meal!).

This paragraph explains the title, and is the key to the story. How exactly does a robot with a compassion circuit differ from an ordinary robot? p. 26

A robot without a compassion circuit simply obeys orders from human beings without in any way questioning them. A robot with a compassion circuit does not automatically obey orders, because its master or mistress may be unwell, and not always behave rationally.

Consequently, the robot weighs up whether a request is good for the patient (on compassionate grounds) or not, and acts accordingly.

p. 26

Why do you think the author included this minor incident?

To show that it is becoming more and more natural for relatively weak human beings to enlist the help of strong robots/rely on robots, perhaps with dangerous consequences in the long term.

p. 26

What does it imply when the author writes **the** screwdriver rather than **a** screwdriver?

It implies that there is only one screwdriver in general use in the house, rather than a number of screwdrivers (of different sizes/ types).

p. 26

Think of as many reasons as you can for emphasising that the robot is a) perfect and b) cold.

a)
- Even the most beautiful human being is not perfect.
- Hester is perfect but not beautiful (Janet might have been jealous).
- Plastic can be perfect, people can't.

b)
- Slightly shocking to touch something which looks human but feels cold (association with dead bodies).
- Reminds us that the robot is not in fact human.
- Helps Janet to remember (for the moment) that the robot is just a machine or "a big doll".

p. 27

How do husband and wife differ in their attitudes to the robot?

The husband has a matter-of-fact, technical attitude to the robot, while the wife already sees it as very close to human, and does not like the idea of her husband undoing its/her blouse, or the fact that there is an opening control panel on the robot's back.

p. 27

What consequences could these differences have later?

It is likely that the husband will continue to make a clear distinction between robots and human beings, but the wife may start to see the robot as a person.

p. 27

How would a *stage parlourmaid* look?

The traditional uniform is black, short, waisted dress (long dress in Victorian times), black stockings and shoes, with a white, starched apron and cap. Most men find this outfit sexy.

p. 28

Which sentences tell the reader that Janet has come to think of Hester as human – even better than human?

In four months ...
From the first ...
The time she couldn't stop walking in a circle ...
Hester was not only a person ...

Is this statement true (that human beings are "accidental")?

p. 28

It is certainly true that many babies are conceived by accident, but Hester has chosen to ignore the long process which has led to the evolution of *homo sapiens*. If we accept Darwin's "survival of the fittest" (= best suited to the environment) theory, then we are not accidental at all.

I don't think I would hesitate ... Can you imagine how the story goes on?

p. 28

Students might be expected to guess that Janet would like to become more like a robot (reliable, strong, easily repaired) in some way.

What do you make of the robot's use of *he* here?

p. 29

It possibly shows a certain lack of respect for George, and also suggests a kind of "girls together" attitude – almost a conspiracy against the husband.

Comment on Janet's new attitude to the robot's coldness.

p. 29

As she has come to like and rely on Hester so much, she is no longer bothered by the fact that the robot feels cold to the touch – on the contrary. She may even prefer this coldness to human warmth.

"It's almost like ..." Can you finish the sentence for George?

p. 31

... a robot('s hand)."

Why *Janet's head?*

p. 31

Because this is the only part of Janet which is still human. The rest of her is a robot.

How can Hester be so sure that Janet will sign the form of consent?

p. 31

As Janet is now a robot herself except for her head, it will obviously solve a lot of problems for her if her husband (whose head is not injured) ends up in the same state.

Activities

1. Why do you think Janet is so ready to accept Hester as a human being?

Reading between the lines p. 31

- She is in a physically and mentally fragile state, and needs someone to talk to, look after her, etc.
- She needs a sympathetic audience (her husband is out at work all day, and may not be a particularly good listener).
- Hester looks human, and because of the compassion circuit, also seems to behave like a sympathetic friend.

2. What evidence can you find in the story for a robot conspiracy?

- Hester arranges Janet's operation with other robots at the hospital.

- She does not consult George first.
- The hospital robot persuades George to sign the form of consent.
- George never gets to see a human doctor.
- He is not allowed to visit Janet in the hospital.
- It is very easy for Hester to arrange the second operation.

3. What form might this conspiracy take?

As robots became more and more efficient, they would be able to go about their work with and less and less outside (human) influence/interference/supervision. As they sensed their power and became aware of the lack of supervision (they would no doubt be good with computers, etc.) they might begin to use their power in ways which suited their purposes rather than ours. The most likely form of conspiracy would be for robots in responsible positions (police, in hospitals, etc.) to start working together. There could be a gradual change from on the whole harmless effects to something like a takeover. If humans protested, the appeal judge would turn out to be a robot, too.

Comprehension – *your* question p. 31

What questions would you ask to check whether another reader has understood the story? Try your questions out on your neighbour, or your fellow-students.

Sample questions:
1. Why does Janet need a robot?
2. What is special about Hester?
3. How does the relationship between Janet and Hester develop?
4. How does Hester feel about human bodies compared with robots?
5. Why does Hester send Janet to hospital?
6. Why can't George find out exactly what is going on?
7. What happens when Janet gets home from hospital?

Ethical issues p. 31

Do you think it would be acceptable to create robots which look and behave like human beings? Give reasons for your answer.

For:
- We expect people in service occupations (shop assistants, waiters, etc.) to **look** human, and would be put off if robots doing these jobs did not look the part.
- On the whole human beings are well equipped physically for doing a very wide range of jobs. It could be counterproductive not to design robots along similar lines.

Against:
- Danger that people would not know whether they were dealing with a person or a robot – could fall in love with robots, etc.
- Robots might be cleverer and better-looking than people, with unpredictable consequences (robot rage – cf. road rage – attacks on robots, etc.)

Robots and "spare parts surgery" in the real world p. 31/32

1. Find out as much as you can about industrial robots. What forms do they take, and in what areas have they replaced human beings?

Students should be encouraged to find out about the use of robots in car production, warehousing, and in dangerous environments, for example.

2. Why do you think domestic robots are taking such a long time to appear in our homes?

It is in fact extremely difficult to design a robot which can do all the jobs a traditional housewife was expected to perform. We are closer to "one-function" robots such as automatic vacuum cleaners. However, even the humble coffee maker or toaster can be seen as a kind of simple robot.

3. Write a short paragraph about the replacement of defective human body parts with human tissue or man-made "spare parts".

Some ideas which students could follow up:
- heart/kidney etc. replacements and the problems which occur, e.g. rejection of alien tissue
- actual replacements of human hands with hands from donors
- hip replacements (finding suitable materials)
- wooden legs, hooks for hands, etc.
- advanced modern artificial limbs
- Will there ever be replacement eyes/ears for blind/deaf people? How far has research progressed towards these age-old dreams?

Write your own "Humans versus robots" story.

◀ Creative writing p. 32

Some ideas:
- Robots win a war for humans then turn on them.
- Humans become degenerate because there is nothing left for them to do.
- Robots compete in sporting events and beat human athletes.
- Robots decide to use humans as their servants.
- Human-robot love affair.
- Humans and robots unite to repel aliens.

Snow Crash 1: Y.T. on her Skateboard Neal Stephenson

Author

Neal Stephenson (*1960) is a highly-respected author of novels which really go beyond science fiction in their dramatic and highly creative evocation of virtual or fictional worlds. *Snow Crash* (1992) ranks with *Brave New World* in its treatment of new technologies. *The Diamond Age* and *The Cobweb* followed. His latest novel, *Cryptonomicon* (1999) deals with the world of codes and code-breakers during WW2 and in the near future. In addition it describes the setting up of a single data bank for the whole world. William Gibson's *Neuromancer* (1984) should be mentioned here as the pioneer cyberspace novel to which later writers on this theme, including Stephenson, are indebted.

About the text

The first extract from *Snow Crash* was chosen because Y.T. is the kind of girl students should find it easy to identify with. The description of her attempt to get a lift from a so-called bimbo box (cheap car for housewives) is both amusing and exciting. Incidental details throw a good deal of light on Stephenson's vision of America in the future. The vision is dystopian, but somehow appealing nevertheless.

Synopsis of the text

The text begins with an advertisement for Y.T's high tech skateboard, which has special rimless wheels with telescopic spokes which can cope very well with rough terrain. She cruises down a hill with the pizza she has to deliver within the next few minutes, looking for a car she can attach her magnetic harpoon to, so that she can travel faster. The car she chooses is just pulling away from the curb. It is a cheap vehicle which has very little steel in it apart from the frame and floor pan, so she has to fling her magnetic harpoon from very near the ground so that it attaches itself to the underside of the car.

Unterrichtsempfehlungen

Die einführenden Erläuterungen auf S. 32 helfen den Schülern, sich in den Kontext der Romanauszüge einzufinden.
Die Aufgabe „Nothing is perfect“ kann unter Einbeziehung der „Werbeanzeige“ auf S. 33 eine Brücke zum ersten Romanauszug „Y.T. on her Skateboard“ spannen. Im Rahmen dieser Aufgabe ist es möglich, die Kursteilnehmer zusätzlich einen ähnlichen Werbetext zu den von ihnen erdachten Verbesserungen von Fahrrädern, Skateboards und Autos etc. verfassen zu lassen.
Da der Text einen nicht unerheblichen Steilheitsgrad aufweist, ist – abhängig von der Leistungsstärke des Kurses – daran zu denken, den Text sprachlich vorzuentlasten. Dies mag von einem oder zwei Schülern/Schülerinnen durchgeführt werden, die dabei als Vokabelexperten auftreten. Unter Berücksichtigung der Anmerkungen am Rand können zu Vokabeln des Textes einfache Zeichnungen entworfen oder Umschreibungen gesucht werden. Ferner wäre es interessant, einige Vokabelbeispiele aus dem Text auszuwählen, die dann vom Plenum aus dem Kontext heraus erschlossen werden.
Eine alternative Herangehensweise wäre ein vorbereitendes Lesen in Kleingruppen. Die Schülerinnen und Schüler werden dabei in die Lage versetzt, sich gegenseitig zu helfen und gemeinsam den Textinhalt zu erfassen. Es bietet sich in diesem Zusammenhang an, mit den Kursteilnehmern Strategien zu wiederholen, um einen unbekannten Text möglichst ohne Wörterbuch zu erschließen.
Mit Hilfe der *while-reading tasks* und den *Activities* kann im Anschluss die weitere Arbeit mit dem Romanauszug erfolgen. Die *Activities* sind so gestaltet, dass sie sich leicht an abwechslungsreiche Aktionsformen knüpfen lassen.

Assignments

Pre-reading task

Try to think of some ways in which common machines (bikes, skateboards, cars, etc.) could be improved. Use your imagination.

Nothing is perfect p. 32

Some ideas:
- bikes – comfort could be improved (springing for touring bikes)
- skateboards – little motors, ability to deal with rough surfaces
- cars – smaller, more economical, less pollution, advanced navigation systems
- trains – better crash-prevention, better services to reduce the number of lorries/trucks on the road
- planes – less pollution, vertical take-off making large airports unnecessary, less noise

While-reading tasks

What kind of text do you think this is? Where is the evidence?

p. 33

Obviously an advertising text:
- detailed and very favourable information about the product
- dangers of inferior products – "total face retread"
- typical appeal to the potential buyer – "upgrade today"

Can you explain the letters D, R and N as used here?

p. 33

They refer to the various options of an automatic gearbox.
D = drive, R = reverse and N = neutral

Explain why the car was parked right up against the curb.

p. 34

Stephenson describes, in an amusingly exaggerated way, how other people, particularly the (female) driver's own children, will make fun of anyone who parks untidily a few inches from the curb. Drivers therefore prefer to grind their tyres against the curb to make sure the car is close enough.

Explain how a superconducting poon would work.

p. 34

It would induce/set up electric eddy currents in non-magnetic metals such as aluminium so that this material is turned into an electromagnet to which the poon will be attracted.

Why does Y.T. need to attack the bimbo box from below?

p. 34

Because this is the only part of the car where there is a reasonable amount of steel to which her poon will stick.

Activities

Present and future
p. 34

1. What features of this world are
   a) not so different from our world
   b) much more advanced?

a) pizza deliveries, suburban houses and gardens, police cars (?), family cars/minivans, parking habits
b) design and use of skateboards, night vision goggles, (magnetic) harpoons.

2. What features are unpleasant, potentially dystopian?

- severe penalties for delivering a pizza late
- police who seem possibly too powerful, threatening
- poor quality dogfood with "undigestible food coloring"
- traditional housewife role has survived unchanged

A question of words
p. 34

The author clearly enjoys using unusual and/or dramatic vocabulary. Pick out some examples and try to explain the effect which they are likely to have on the reader.

e.g.
total face retread – the reader will imagine the skateboarder sliding along the ground on his/her face so that all the skin (and more!) is removed.
to glom,'crete, lambada – unusual and interesting words or versions of words which will help the reader to imagine this different world.
bimbo box – the term is amusing. The deliberate sexism does not mean that the author is sexist, only that this future world has not overcome its prejudices.

Creative writing
p. 34

Either imagine how the driver of the car (it's a teenager not a housewife) might try to get rid of Y.T. and write a racy description in a similar style to Stephenson's ...

Some ideas:
- could accelerate very fast
- or brake hard so that Y.T. runs into the back of the car
- or take a corner very fast, hoping centrifugal force will break the magnetic link between car and poon
- or take a tight turn around a lamppost, hoping that Y.T.s cable will get tangled round it – or that she will hit the post

... **or** imagine that Y.T's skateboard is available here and now. Write an interview between a policeman and a boy or girl he has caught using it on our roads (don't forget the poon).

Possible start:
P: Good evening, miss. I suppose you know you're breaking the law.
G: Er, no. I was just out for an evening ride.
P: Which involved throwing things at passing motorists.
G: Oh, no, You've got it wrong, officer. This thing just sticks to cars. It doesn't do any damage. Look – it sticks to your police car.
P: Hey, stop that ...

Snow Crash 2: The Metaverse

Neal Stephenson

About the text

Stephenson's description of the Metaverse is of high literary quality, and takes readers into a virtual reality world more advanced and fascinating than anything which exists at present, although progress in this area is incredibly fast. Students should be interested in the whole concept, and also in the idea that people move around and communicate in the Metaverse as avatars which they can design themselves.

Synopsis of the text

Hiro is approaching the main street in the Metaverse, which is rather like a virtual version of Las Vegas (see the photograph on p. 37). Building work and demolition take place as in the real world, but here everything is generated by computer software. It is always nighttime in the Metaverse, but the Street (normal way of referring to it) is always brilliantly lit. There is a free monorail service down the middle. Before this was built, pioneers like Hiro wrote themselves car and motorcycle software in order to get around. Hiro describes two young couples who have arrived in the Metaverse for an evening out. In reality they will be sitting at home with their laptops. They don't talk to Hiro because his avatar is expensive and dangerous-looking. Stephenson explains how an avatar can look like anything you want it to, as long as you can afford it. Three of the four young people have bought standard, unsubtle off-the-shelf avatars, but one of the girls has built herself quite a nice customized one from a construction kit.

Unterrichtsempfehlungen

Durch die Erarbeitung des ersten Romanauszugs dürften die Schülerinnen und Schüler mit dem Sprachstil Stephensons vertraut sein. Die Lektüre des Textes „The Metaverse" dürfte daher weniger Schwierigkeiten bereiten.
Die Fotografie „Las Vegas at night" auf Seite 37 bietet sich als Einstimmung auf die Welt „Metaverse" an und kann gut im Anschluss an die Fragen „What do you know about virtual reality?" und „How is it already being used?" betrachtet werden. Die Schülerinnen und Schüler formulieren in einem kurzen Statement, welche Assoziationen und Gefühle bei der Betrachtung der Fotografie in ihnen aufsteigen.
In einem alternativen Verfahren hält der Kurs das Schülerbuch geschlossen, während der Lehrer oder die Lehrerin die ersten fünf Zeilen des Textes auf Folie präsentiert. Der Kurs stellt in Bezug auf den Text Vermutungen über den Fortgang des Handlungsgeschehens an und spekuliert darüber, welche Erlebnisse die Welt des „Metaverse" für Hiro und andere Teilnehmer bereithalten könnte.
Nach der vollständigen Lektüre des Textes können die Arbeitsanweisungen auf Seite 37 angegangen werden.
Im Rahmen der „Key terms" wäre es interessant, die Textproduktionen einmal Personen vorzulesen, denen „The Metaverse" unbekannt ist (z.B. Schülerinnen und Schülern eines Parallelkurses

oder einer anderen Jahrgangsstufe). Nachfolgend sollte überprüft werden, inwieweit das von den „Gasthörern“ durch die Schülerprodukte gewonnene Verständnis der Begriffe „avators“ und „Metaverse“ mit Stephensons Ausführungen übereinstimmt. Es wird so ein Prozess initiiert, welcher unweigerlich zu einer weiteren intensiven Auseinandersetzung mit dem Text führt.
Die zweite Aufgabe „Your avator“ ließe sich von den Kursteilnehmerinnen und Kursteilnehmern zu Hause bearbeiten. Denkbar wäre, dass die Schüler ihre Texte nicht handschriftlich, sondern in Maschinenschrift anfertigen. Bei der Hausaufgabenpräsentation werden die Texte dann eingesammelt, gemischt und wieder ausgeteilt. Den Schülerinnen und Schülern fällt die Aufgabe zu, anhand der Hinweise aus dem Text zu vermuten, welches Kursmitglied hinter dem jeweiligen „avator“ steht. Diese affektiv-emotionale Methode trägt sicherlich ein wenig dazu bei, die Mitschüler einmal aus einem anderen Blickwinkel wahrnehmen zu können.
„A seductive virtual world“ kann in Gruppen diskutiert werden, wobei jede Gruppe ihre Pro- und Kontraargumente stichpunktartig notieren sollte. Hier bietet es sich wieder an, immer nur ein Argument in angemessener Schriftgröße auf ein Blatt Papier zu notieren, damit später die Ergebnisse aller Gruppen übersichtlich an die Tafel geheftet werden können. So können innerhalb des Plenums sämtliche Pro- und Kontraargumente in den Blick genommen werden und auf ihre Stichhaltigkeit bzw. Überzeugungskraft hin untersucht werden.
Der den Aufgabenapparat abschließende Schreibanlass „The role of SF“ ermöglicht es, die im Rahmen des Kapitels mit SF-Literatur gemachten Erfahrungen einzubringen. Selbstverständlich können hier auch ganz individuelle Vorlieben und Abneigungen berücksichtigt werden.
Die Ergebnisse dieser Aufgabe können zudem zur schlüssigen Weiterarbeit an dem „Project“ (S. 38) genutzt werden – die daraus hervorgehenden Produkte, zusammengefasst in einem Heft oder kleinem Buch, lassen sich bei schulischen Veranstaltungen präsentieren und verkaufen. Zu Gelegenheiten wie Schulfesten, Projekttagen oder dem „Tag der offenen Tür“ wäre auch an Autorenlesungen zu denken, bei denen die Schülerinnen und Schüler ihre Texte sprechgestalterisch vor einem Publikum umsetzen.

Assignments

Pre-reading task

Before you read p. 35

What do you know about *virtual reality*? How is it already being used?

Students should know that it is possible to create very realistic or futuristic scenarios via computers. One normally enters the virtual world with the help of special goggles.
Virtual reality is already being used to give potential customers a realistic idea of what their new kitchen or living room could look like.

They can "walk" around, looking at the units/furniture from different angles, and of course rearrange the different items to see which arrangement suits them best.

While-reading tasks

What do you make of this last feature?

p. 35

It suggests that there will always be plenty of people who are potentially violent. Perhaps football hooligans may get the violence out of their systems in a virtual world one day, instead of fighting one another in the real streets, with all the attendant bloodshed and damage to property.

Comment on the language of the sentence beginning "They would take ..."

p. 35

The language is very poetic. Stevenson successfully conveys the excitement Metaverse pioneers would have felt as they raced their virtual bikes and cars out into the black desert beyond the street.

Activities

Write a paragraph each on the terms the *Metaverse* and *avatars* as used by the author.

Key terms
p. 37

Points that could be made:
Metaverse:
- a virtual street
- it is always night there
- people can "build" houses (and clubs, discos, etc.) there
- very brightly lit
- an interesting place to spend an evening
- free monorail service
- people appear in the Metaverse as avatars

Avatars:
- visible form people take in the Metaverse
- they can choose any form they like
- customized forms are expensive and hard to create
- it is possible to buy standard, rather crude designs off the shelf
- or construct a rather more subtle and lifelike avatar from a construction kit
- avatars can communicate with one another as in real life

If it was possible to design your own avatar, what would it be like?

Your avatar
p. 37

There are some good ideas in the text which students can develop.

For some people the Metaverse might simply provide a bit of harmless fun. For others it could become dangerously addictive, and/or be used as an escape from reality, almost as if it were a drug. Argue the case for and against this kind of virtual reality world, making your position clear. How do your fellow-students feel about it?

A seductive virtual world
p. 37

Points for:
- interesting/exciting
- escape from one's own physical appearance/limitations
- available to anyone with a computer, unlike real big city entertainments
- can communicate with people you would never meet in real life

Points against:
- people do not move from their sofas while in the Metaverse – will become couch potatoes – unhealthy
- success in the Metaverse is meaningless in the real world
- easy to become addicted
- probable depression when people return to unpromising surroundings/prospects in the real world
- depressing for people who are not physically attractive when they leave their avatars, which will probably have been made very attractive to compensate

The role of SF p. 37

Neal Stephenson is seen as an author who cannot only imagine what the future might be like, but also describe both good and bad aspects in a dramatic way. Write a paragraph in which you discuss potential functions of good SF writing.

Some points which could be made:
- can "stretch" the imagination
- good entertainment
- can enable us to visualise/comprehend what the future may be like more powerfully than a dry scientific report would be able to do
- can even help us to save ourselves from undesirable developments by describing the dangers in a graphic way (dystopian literature)
- poor SF consists of hackneyed adventure stories with a futuristic setting. Good SF writers create fictional worlds which go far beyond this and may help us to imagine how our world could be improved (utopian elements in the more favourable sense of the word)
- can help us to imagine what life might be like for other intelligent species/on other planets

Additional texts

Cloning Dinosaurs Michael Crichton

"It's not an ordinary zoo," Dodgson said. "This zoo is unique in the world. It seems that InGen has done something quite extraordinary. They have managed to clone extinct animals from the past."
"What animals?"
"Animals that hatch from eggs, and that require a lot of room in a zoo."
"What animals?"
"Dinosaurs," Dodgson said. "They are cloning dinosaurs." [...]
In fact, there had been discussion of cloning dinosaurs in the technical literature as far back as 1982. With each passing year, the mani-

pulation of DNA had grown easier. Genetic material had already been extracted from Egyptian mummies, and from the hide of a quagga, a zebra-like African animal that had become extinct in the 1880s. By 1985, it seemed possible that quagga DNA might be reconstituted, and a new animal grown. If so, it would be the first creature brought back from extinction solely by reconstruction of its DNA. If that was possible, what else was also possible? The mastodon? The saber-toothed tiger? The dodo?

Or even a dinosaur?

Of course, no dinosaur DNA was known to exist anywhere in the world. But by grinding up large quantities of dinosaur bones it might be possible to extract fragments of DNA. Formerly it was thought that fossilization eliminated all DNA. Now that was recognized as untrue. If enough DNA fragments were recovered, it might be possible to clone a living animal.

Back in 1982, the technical problems hat seemed daunting. But there was no theoretical barrier. It was merely difficult, expensive, and unlikely to work. Yet it was certainly possible, if anyone cared to try.

InGen had apparently decided to try.

"What they have done," Dodgson said, "is build the greatest single tourist attraction in the history of the world. As you know, zoos are extremely popular. Last year, more Americans visited zoos than all professional baseball and football games combined. And the Japanese love zoos – there are fifty zoos in Japan, and more being built. And for this zoo, InGen can charge whatever they want. Two thousand dollars a day, ten thousand dollars a day ... And then there is the *merchandising*. The picture books, T-shirts, video games, caps, stuffed toys, comic books, and pets."

"Pets?"

"Of course. If InGen can make full-size dinosaurs, they can also make pygmy dinosaurs as household pets. What child won't want a little dinosaur as a pet? A little patented animal for their very own. InGen will sell millions of them. And InGen will engineer them so that these pet dinosaurs can only eat InGen pet food. ..."

"Jesus," somebody said.

"Exactly," Dodgson said. "The zoo is the centerpiece of an enormous enterprise."

"You said these dinosaurs will be patented?"

"Yes. Genetically engineered animals can now be patented. The Supreme Court ruled on that in favor of Harvard in 1987. InGen will own its dinosaurs, and no one else can legally make them."

The Bicentennial Man Isaac Asimov

The Three Laws of Robotics:

1. *A robot may not injure a human being or, through inaction, allow a human being to come to harm.*
2. *A robot must obey the orders given it by human beings except where such orders would conflict with the First Law.*
3. *A robot must protect its own existence as long as such protection does not conflict with the First or Second Law.*

1.

Andrew Martin said, “Thank you,” and took the seat offered him. He didn’t look driven to the last resort, but he had been.

He didn’t, actually, look anything, for there was a smooth blankness to his face, except for the sadness one imagined one saw in his eyes. His hair was smooth, light brown, rather fine, and there was no facial hair. He looked freshly and cleanly shaved. His clothes were distinctly old-fashioned, but neat and predominantly a velvety redpurple in color.

Facing him from behind the desk was the surgeon, and the name-plate on the desk included a fully identifying series of letters and numbers, which Andrew didn’t bother with. To call him Doctor would be quite enough.

“When can the operation be carried through, Doctor?” he asked.

The surgeon said softly, with that certain inalienable note of respect that a robot always used to a human being. “I am not certain, sir, that I understand how or upon whom such an operation could be performed.”

There might have been a look of respectful intransigence on the surgeon’s face, if a robot of his sort, in lightly bronzed stainless steel, could have such an expression, or any expression.

Andrew Martin studied the robot’s right hand, his cutting hand, as it lay on the desk in utter tranquillity. The fingers were long and shaped into artistically metallic looping curves so graceful and appropriate that one could imagine a scalpel fitting them and becoming, temporarily, one piece with them.

There would be no hesitation in his work, no stumbling, no quivering, no mistakes. That came with specialization, of course, a specialization so fiercely desired by humanity that few robots were, any longer, independently brained. A surgeon, of course, would have to be. And this one, though brained, was so limited in his capacity that he did not recognize Andrew – had probably never heard of him.

Andrew said, “Have you ever thought you would like to be a man?”

The surgeon hesitated a moment as though the question fitted nowhere in his allotted positronic pathways. “But I am a robot, sir.”

“Would it be better to be a man?”

“It would be better, sir, to be a better surgeon. I could not be so if I were a man, but only if I were a more advanced robot. I would be pleased to be a more advanced robot.”

“It does not offend you that I can order you about? That I can make you stand up, sit down, move right or left, by merely telling you to do so?”

“It is my pleasure to please you, sir. If your orders were to interfere with my functioning with respect to you or to any other human being, I would not obey you. The First Law, concerning my duty to human safety, would take precedence over the Second Law relating to obedience. Otherwise, obedience is my pleasure. ... But upon whom an I to perform this operation?”

“Upon me,” said Andrew.

“But that is impossible. It is patently a damaging operation.”

“That does not matter,” said Andrew calmly.

“I must not inflict damage,” said the surgeon.

“On a human being, you must not,” said Andrew, “but I, too, am a robot.”

Chapter 3: Challenges and Dangers

Vorbemerkungen zum Kapitel

Im Zentrum des abschließenden Kapitels stehen vornehmlich Sachtexte, wobei *ein* Schwerpunkt auf dem Bereich der „environmental issues“ liegt. Hier können sowohl die individuellen Haltungen der Schülerinnen und Schüler gegenüber Fragen des Umweltschutzes thematisiert, als auch Ursachen und Auswirkungen von Umweltverschmutzungen in globalen Zusammenhängen diskutiert werden.

Start here

Unterrichtsempfehlungen

Der Cartoon zum Einstieg in das neue Kapitel kann zunächst ohne den Text vom Lehrenden auf Folie präsentiert werden. In Kleingruppen verfassen die Schülerinnen und Schüler dann dazu eigene Sprechblasen. Anschließend notiert der Lehrer/die Lehrerin die Produkte der Gruppen auf Folie, wobei die Schülerinnen und Schüler anhand des Bildes den Text ihrer Sprechblasen begründen sollten. Danach lässt sich der Originalcartoon im Schülerbuch mit Hilfe der einführenden Fragen auf Seite 39 angehen.
Die Einstellung der Lernenden gegenüber Fragen des Umweltschutzes und die damit einhergehenden widersprüchlichen Verhaltensweisen lassen sich nachfolgend Gewinn bringend in einem offenem Unterrichtsgespräch zur Sprache bringen.
In Partnerarbeit (vgl. Schülerbuch, S. 38 unten) werden danach die Vorzüge neuer Technologien mit ihrer Kehrseite erarbeitet und aufgelistet. Die aus dieser Unterrichtsphase hervorgehenden Kernpunkte sollten an der Tafel festgehalten werden, damit die Schüler ihre eigene Liste ergänzen und vervollständigen können. Auf diese Weise verschaffen sich die Lernenden zu Beginn des neuen Kapitels „Challenges and Dangers“ Klarheit über den eigenen Standpunkt hinsichtlich der Problematik. Im Verlauf der Arbeit an dem Kapitel mit seinen vielfältigen Texten und Abbildungen eröffnet sich für sie dann die Möglichkeit, den eigenen Standpunkt/die eigene Wahrnehmung zu bestätigen, zu erweitern oder aber auch zu hinterfragen und zu verändern.

Back to nature – but in an air-conditioned car, please! p. 39

What do you see as the “message” of the cartoon above?

People from the industrialised countries tend to expect the services/attractions which they have paid for/read about in a holiday brochure to be available as and when announced. They are unwilling to accept that wild animals, for example, will not necessarily be prepared to “play ball”/ co-operate in this way.

Perhaps you can think of some other examples of illogical behaviour.

e.g.
- Driving a long way to buy slightly cheaper petrol
- "Camping" in a luxurious motor home
- Distributing millions of plastic sacks in order to help people to recycle plastics.
- Fitting catalytic converters to more and more powerful/thirsty cars as a sop to our consciences
- Driving to a fitness centre and then riding an exercise bike
- Using precious fresh water to flush toilets

Work with your fellow-students to produce a list of recent technological advances, along with their advantages and disadvantages as you see them.

Some of the options:

modern diesel engines	very powerful and economical	dangerous soot particles
flying for everyone	cheap holidays, mobility	noise and air pollution
pesticides, fertilisers	efficient food production	cocktail of powerful chemicals in our food
modern life-saving techniques	people survive serious accidents	some survive only as "vegetables", unnecessary in many cases
mobile phones	total communication	irritating for other people

The Dangers of Cloning Aisling Irwin

About the text

Richard Dawkins enjoys being deliberately provocative. It is possible that he does not really hold some of the extreme views expressed in the article, but they should spark off reactions among students.

Synopsis of the text

The author is reporting on a radio interview with Prof. Richard Dawkins. Dawkins claimed that he would be quite happy to clone his own daughter. He saw no difference in principle between cloning in the laboratory and identical twins, which are natural clones. He would have no objection to cloning his favourite dog so that the clone could live on after the dog itself died. He believed people's objections to cloning were irrational. Cloning could help childless couples to have a family. He would even like to be able to make a copy of himself, fifty years younger.

Unterrichtsempfehlungen

Der recht kurze, jedoch inhaltlich sehr provokante Text „The dangers of cloning" kann im Unterricht gelesen werden. Durch Erarbeitung der ersten beiden Aufgaben der *Activities* lassen sich die Kernthesen Dawkins kritisch beleuchten.
Im Zusammenhang mit der Arbeit am Text bieten sich ferner Möglichkeiten für eine Zusammenarbeit mit anderen Fachbereichen an

(Religion, Biologie – vgl. Unterrichtsempfehlungen zu Kapitel 2, „Brave New World"). Der zweite Teil des Aufgabenapparats („Ethics") ließe sich beispielsweise in Kooperation mit dem Religionskurs angehen.
Die schriftliche Aufgabe „Personal opinions" sollte in häuslicher Arbeit ausgeführt werden.

Assignments

While-reading task

Are pets different from people when it comes to cloning?

p. 40

Sample answer:
People were fascinated by the cloning of a sheep, and would certainly be interested in the idea that pets could be cloned. A few people might be shocked, but others would see how children, for example, could be spared the unhappiness which the death of a favourite pet causes. However, cloning human beings raises complex ethical, moral and religious issues and would be extremely controversial, to say the least.

Activities

1. Make a list of the main statements attributed to Dawkins in the article

Notes p. 40

He would not necessarily object to having his daughter cloned
- identical twins are clones
- he would be delighted to have a cherished labrador cloned
- human cloning could help some childless couples
- he found the idea that he could make a younger copy of himself fascinating.

2. Discuss them with your partner. Is Dawkins right, wrong, or just trying to provoke people?

Some useful gambits for student comments:
- Do you think he really believes ...
- I agree with Dawkins up to a point, but ...
- No one really thinks/believes ...
- How would you feel if ...
- There's one thing I'm sure he's right/wrong about ...

Dawkins has been described as a *renowned anti-religion campaigner.* How might someone with strong religious views react to these statements?

Ethics p. 40

Sample answer:
Dawkins does not mention God at any point, so he clearly would not allow religious considerations to influence his views. A religious person would want to point out a number of powerful reasons for approaching the cloning of human beings with extreme care, e.g.

- Each human being is unique.
- Human beings are made by God, not man.
- Human beings have a soul – would this apply to a clone?
- We should not interfere with God's work.
- We do not have the right to perpetuate ourselves by cloning.

Personal opinions ➤ p. 40

Write a paragraph expressing your own views on human and animal cloning.

Students' personal opinions. Plenty of suitable material is available above and in the text.
Some gambits which will help students to write a coherent text:

– on the whole	– nevertheless
– however	– on the one/the other hand
– in my view	– taking everything into account
– at times	– finally

Non-human Communication

Celia Brayfield

About the text

The author has written a deliberately overstated argument in favour of traditional person to person communication. She makes much use of dramatic examples in order to demonstrate how far we have travelled in what she sees as the wrong direction, towards more and more virtual communication, which is leading to increasing alienation from other members of our species.

Synopsis of the text

The first example the author uses to back up her claim that we are losing contact with one other is the advice given by an American business expert that we should introduce a "human moment" into the working day. She goes on to claim that e-mails and answering machines are taking away our social skills, and making us afraid of real human contacts. Her next example is the teenage computer addict who would once have gone to the school dance, but now communicates with girls via chat rooms. The trend is the same in other areas. People do not want to go to office parties, and salesmen are unable to function without a programme to follow. Even very small children can become so addicted to video games that nothing else matters to them.
Finding a partner is a question of searching the net for someone with the right set of desirable attributes. In the long run children are likely to suffer most from these developments.

Unterrichtsempfehlungen

„Non-human Communication" warnt vor der Entfremdung des Menschen durch moderne Kommunikationstechnologien und Arbeitsprozesse. Der Einstieg erfolgt über das Bildmaterial in Zusammenhang mit den darunter abgedruckten Fragen. Insbesondere die Problemstellung "Some people would say that life was better in the 'good old days'. Do you agree ?" verdient dabei Aufmerksamkeit, da die Fotografien möglicherweise zu einer Verall-

gemeinerung (Entfremdung – Zuwendung) verführen können. Eine Romantisierung der Arbeitswelt der ersten Hälfte des 20. Jahrhunderts würde dieser jedoch nicht gerecht. Lärm und teilweise extrem große körperliche Belastung in den Produktionsstätten schlossen ausgiebige Gespräche zwischen Arbeitern sicherlich aus. Es ist beachtenswert, dass eine Fotografie einen Angestellten bei der Arbeit zeigt, während die andere Frauen mit einem Kind in einer Pausensituation abbildet. Bei dieser Gelegenheit ließe sich noch einmal das Rollenverständnis von Frauen in der so genannten „guten alten Zeit" thematisieren (vgl. „Compassion Circuit", S. 25).
Nach dieser hinführenden Phase kann der Artikel von Brayfield in Einzelarbeit gelesen werden, wobei die Schülerinnen und Schüler sich Notizen zur Beantwortung der *while-reading tasks* machen sollten. Nachfolgend können diese dann ausgewertet werden. Eine vertiefende Erschließungsarbeit kann anhand der ersten Fragen der *Activities* vorgenommen werden. Die aus der ersten Aufgabe hervorgehenden Ergebnisse sollten dabei stichpunktartig an der Tafel festgehalten werden.
In Anspielung auf den Titel des gesamten Themenhefts ließen sich im Rahmen von „Another view" die Risiken, aber auch Chancen neuer Kommunikationstechnologien diskutieren. Die oftmals anzutreffende Neigung, ausschließlich die Risiken neuer Technologien zu betonen, kann hier durch eine differenzierte Sichtweise ersetzt werden.

Assignments

Pre-reading task

Losing the human touch? p. 41

Describe the scenes in the photographs. When do you think each of them was taken? Some people would say that life was better in the "good old days." Do you agree? How did people communicate in those days? Did they have more time for one another? How do you feel about life in the modern office as depicted in the second photograph? What is the function of the CCTV (closed circuit television) equipment?

The first scene is a famous black and white photograph, taken around the middle of the twentieth century, judging by the clothes the women and the little boy are wearing. The housing is typical terraced housing of the type which used to exist in most British cities. Two women are chatting "over the garden fence". They clearly have plenty of time for their chat, and the little boy is included. We can safely assume that they are housewives whose husbands are out at work, doing manual jobs. The photo was taken to show a working class version of the good life *(Heile Welt)*.
The picture is idealised. Some aspects of the "good old days" may really have been good (sense of community etc.), but standards of living were low, and workers were often treated badly by employers. Few people had telephones in those days. They communicated by

going to see one another and only used (public) telephones/sent telegrams in an emergency.
The office worker in the second photograph is alone at his desk, and clearly under stress (bottle of pills). His work involves dealing with material which comes to him via the computer screen. He has become a cog in a non-human machine. The CCTV equipment is there to monitor him – Big Brother tendencies. He wears an identity badge in order to gain access to restricted areas, and/or because people in big modern organisations often don't know one another. However, he is allowed to dress casually for work. Collar and tie are unfashionable in most IT (information technology) companies.

While-reading tasks

p. 42 ➤

What do you think this term (psychobabble) means?

Psychobabble is the use of terms from psycho-analysis in ordinary conversation. The idea is to say quite ordinary things in a way that sounds impressive. *Babble* implies that the terms lose most of their meaning when used like this.

p. 42 ➤

Can you name and explain the figure of speech?

The figure of speech is a simile. Just as moss crept across the fields of Ireland and made them infertile, so alienation is creeping into our lives and killing real human communication/face to face interaction.

p. 43 ➤

Can you explain the joke at the end of the article?

Many telephone services now allow users to access the information they require via the dialling buttons on their telephones. However, this information is normally given in recorded form. It is often very hard to make contact with a real person. In the incident described, pressing a button is very unlikely to stop the town being terrorised.

Activities

The way we live now p. 43 ➤

1. Make a list of the dangers for humanity which are referred to in the article.

- So little real communication takes place in (some) offices that a "human moment" is needed.
- People don't believe standardised messages thanking them for their order.
- E-mails are an impoverished form of communication (politeness, thanks, etc. are a waste of screen space).
- Teenagers become couch potatoes "meeting" members of the opposite sex in chat rooms, afraid of real human contact.
- PR people say no one will go to parties.
- Sales executives can't think on their feet any more. They need a programme to help them.
- It is hard to find receptionists who can say hello and smile.
- At least one child plays video games all day long and regards anything else as an unwelcome interruption.

- People don't fall in love any more. Instead they have checklists of desirable attributes and look for the "right" partner on the internet.

2. Explain in your own words exactly why these modern trends are so dangerous.

All these trends are reducing person to person contact and making us afraid of actually meeting and talking to one another. The result is likely to be a loveless world in which people sit alone in front of their computer screens, taking part in virtual communication instead of the real thing. The key word is alienation (from other members of our species). Some people deliberately phone acquaintances when they know the speech partner is at work because they prefer to talk to the answering machine.

3. Comment on the way little Sam is being brought up. What problems is he likely to have in later life.

This is an incredible way to bring up a child. Most parents use the television as a baby-minder from time to time, but for Sam, violent video games have become his whole life. Mother love plays no role in his life. He will find it very difficult to form normal human relationships, and is quite likely to become a criminal. Other children will inevitably regard him as an outsider.

What makes us human?
p. 43

"Conversation, charm, empathy, intuition, tolerance and acceptance." Is this a good list of human characteristics? Add/remove items to make your own list and compare it with your neighbour's list.

The answers are entirely up to students here. It would be worth pointing out that there is no mention of more assertive human characteristics, which are also important, e.g. ability to get one's views across to other people, ability to take the initiative, to create, to invent, to question the status quo. There is too much emphasis on "being nice".

Another view
p. 43

How far do you agree with the author of the article, and how far with the student?

Sample answer:
It is certainly true that computers etc. are reducing the amount of face to face human contact, and some jobs have definitely become very impersonal. On the other hand, it is much easier to keep in touch with people via e-mail than writing conventional letters, and the services available on the internet can enrich our lives and widen our horizons if we use them wisely.

A short essay
p. 43

Write a short essay with the title "The computer and I". Try to explain what (if anything) you use a computer for, what problems you have had with computers, whether you enjoy working with a computer, and whether you think you are likely to use a computer more or less in the future.

Typical student uses:
- e-mail
- downloading information
- games
- buying books
- writing essays/papers
- surfing the internet
- chat rooms (?)

Typical problems:
- configuring the system and getting everything working
- computer crashes
- incompatibility between different elements of a system
- "losing" texts one has written
- viruses

Pollution Battle Takes to the Skies

Pat Malone

About the text

The huge increase in air travel for business and pleasure is one of the most striking phenomena of the last twenty years or so. There is a danger that people will accept cheap air travel as a good thing without considering the other side of the coin. The article will open readers' eyes to the hidden costs and dangers.

Synopsis of the text

As air travel grows, so does the amount of pollution which it causes. Warning voices are beginning to be heard, but compared with cars, awareness of pollution by planes is in its infancy. Huge amounts of kerosene are burnt in the troposphere, where the waste products are likely to cause the most damage. 100,000 people are in the air over the North Atlantic at any one time. Britain has 69 Boeing 747's and 200 other jets, but this is next to nothing compared with the US, which has 30 % of all the world's jets flying on domestic services alone. The Pacific Rim countries have the fastest growth rate of all but the danger from former Soviet bloc countries is even greater because they are still flying inefficient, dirty, and out-of-date planes. Aviation is the fastest-growing area of fossil fuel use. There is little incentive to economise because airlines generally use tax-free fuel.
British Airways' Head of Environment questions some of the figures, and claims that his airline is careful with its fuel consumption, which has halved over the past 20 years. Environmental groups disagree. They claim that there are huge hidden subsidies, and that "flying is the most polluting form of transport there is". Huge amounts of revenue would be generated if kerosene were taxed at the same rate as petrol for cars.

Unterrichtsempfehlungen

Für den Einstieg sind zwei unterschiedliche Verfahren denkbar. Zum einen können die Schülerinnen und Schüler der unter der Fotografie abgedruckten Arbeitsanweisung folgend möglichst viele Ursachen für Umweltverschmutzungen zusammentragen und untereinander vergleichen. Es ist denkbar, dass sie ihre Ergebnisse nicht nur mit dem Nachbarn, sondern auch mit anderen im Kurs zu vergleichen, indem sie sich im Raum bewegen, aufeinander zugehen, miteinander sprechen und sich austauschen.
Zum anderen ließe sich eine *mind map* zum Begriff „pollution“ an der Tafel entwickeln. Dabei könnte der Tafelanschrieb und die

Leitung des Unterrichtsgesprächs in dieser Phase von ein bis zwei Schülerinnen oder Schülern übernommen werden. Nach dem Lesen des Textes unter Berücksichtigung der am Rand befindlichen *while-reading tasks* kann im Rahmen von „Clarifying your own view“ (S. 46) exemplarisch verdeutlicht werden, wie wichtig das systematische Sammeln von Ideen und Argumenten vor dem Abfassen eines Textes zu einem bestimmten Thema ist.
Die nachfolgende Anweisung, ein Diagramm schriftlich zu analysieren und zu interpretieren, knüpft unmittelbar an Gegebenheiten der modernen Berufswelt an. Es sind hier nicht nur die immer enger werdenden internationalen Verknüpfungen von Unternehmen mit Sitz in verschiedenen Ländern zu nennen, sondern auch die Tatsache, dass auf nationaler Ebene in bestimmten Abteilungen von Firmen Englisch als Arbeitssprache Verwendung findet (u.a. Ford in Köln).
Die Arbeitsvorschläge zu „Expressing different points of view“ beinhalten eine produktionsorientierte Zielsetzung. Vor dem Verfassen der Dialoge bietet es sich an, mit dem Kurs sprachliche Mittel und Redewendungen (z.B. Well ..., Anyway ..., However ..., You see ..., etc.) zu üben.

Assignments

Pre-reading task

List as many sources of pollution as you can think of in your personal order of seriousness. Compare lists with your neighbours.

Pollution wherever you look p. 44

e.g. air and water pollution from factories, car exhausts, domestic heating systems, planes, chemical spills as a result of vehicle or industrial accidents, anti-fouling paint on ships, pesticides and fertilisers (run-off into rivers, traces in much of what we eat and drink).

While-reading tasks

Explain this use of figurative language.

p. 44

It is as if the car and plane are driving along side by side. The car is slowing down for the red light because motorists are becoming increasingly aware of pollution risks (and the manufacturers are doing quite a lot to reduce pollution – catalytic converters, more efficient engines, better streamlining – at least in Europe), but the plane is overtaking the car/not slowing down (yet) because the same kind of awareness is still in its very early stages.

How many Pacific Rim countries can you name?

p. 45

e.g. the US, Canada, Mexico, China, Hong Kong, Vietnam, Korea, Philippines, Australia, New Zealand, Russia, Colombia, Ecuador, Peru, Chile.

p. 45

About how much is 10p in DM or Euros? Compare kerosene and petrol/diesel prices.

In June 2000 10p was roughly 30 German pfennigs or 15 cents (Euro), and a litre of unleaded super cost over DM 2 – about seven times as expensive.

p. 45

Do you see anything strange about an airline employing a Head of Environment? What would his job be?

As airlines are major polluters, there is something rather strange about them employing a Head of Environment. It is not very likely that someone in this position would actually be involved in cutting down pollution. A cynic would assume that his main job is public relations – putting the most favourable spin on statistics and emphasising all the hard work and research which his company is doing in order to reduce pollution, while the number of subsidised flights on cheap kerosene continues to increase.

p. 45

Would this (more tax revenue) be the only result of more expensive air travel?

Not necessarily. The price of flights would increase, so there might well be less air travel, with more road and rail travel to compensate – with more traffic jams and pollution at ground level as a consequence. However, if less air travel meant more investment in high-speed trains like the Transrapid, this could be a desirable development.

Activities

Clarifying your own view **p. 46**

1. Look at the statements below and arrange them into two columns, for and against air travel. Add some more ideas of your own.

For
Planes are fast. Flying is just great.
Trains need expensive tracks.
Diesel buses are terrible polluters, too.
Air travel is cheap.
Modern cars are clean – soon planes will be, too.
Flying is the twenty-first century way of travelling.
Planes only need a few miles of runway.
Planes are much more efficient nowadays.
Flying is the only sensible way to cross oceans or continents.
We should worry more about trucks on the motorways.

Against
We're wrecking the upper atmosphere.
Flying is not really as cheap as it seems.
Airlines have unfair advantages.
Short flights don't make sense.
No one really knows what affects the ozone layer (could go in either column).

Other ideas:

For

Air travel is safe compared with other means of transport.
No delays at border controls.
Pleasant service on board.
Smooth, quiet travel (as a rule).
Fantastic panoramic views on fine days.

Against

Noise pollution near airports.
When accidents happen, they are usually disastrous.
Airports are usually a long way from town centres – time wasted getting there.
Time wasted at check-in.
Jet lag

Write a paragraph in which you analyse and interpret the information in the graph.

Dealing with graphs p. 46

The graph makes it clear that planes are by far the greatest producers of carbon dioxide (a greenhouse gas) per passenger km, with cars second, and trains and buses bringing up the rear. The picture is different when it comes to poisonous nitrous oxide. Here buses are the main culprits with planes second and cars third. Trains are the easy winners in this category.

1. Imagine that you are talking to a friend who is about to go on a cheap package holiday (travelling by air, of course) to somewhere like Thailand. You have just read this article, and are worried about air pollution caused by planes. How might the conversation go? Write it out and practise it with a partner, so that you can perform it as a playlet.

Expressing different points of view p. 47

Possible start to the playlet:
A: I've just booked a fantastic holiday in Thailand.
B: Good for you – as long as you don't care about the environment.
A: What do you mean? Of course I care about the environment.
B: No, you don't – not if you're going to fly.
A: How else can you get to Thailand? It would take weeks by ship.
B: Perhaps you shouldn't go there at all.
A: What? Why on earth not?
B: Well, ...

2. Now choose one of these pairs of speakers and write another conversation:
   a) yourself and a businessman who is a frequent flyer
   b) yourself and Dr Hugh Somerville
   c) an airline pilot and the driver of a high-speed train.

Some ideas:
a) Businessman points out that he needs to travel fast – no time for leisurely trips. Opponent says high-speed trains are almost as fast within Europe – and how about video-conferencing? Are all those flights really necessary? Stress levels high with frequent travellers. But not if you travel business class and can use the VIP lounges at airports.
b) Somerville claims that BA is already doing a very good job on the environment, and will continue to improve. Opponent says airlines are complacent and enjoy unfair advantages compared with other forms of travel. Somerville denies this – says many of the

statistics used by environmental groups are questionable. Opponent raises controversial issues such as noise and air pollution – suggests that Somerville is not in a position to do anything concrete – really just a PR man. Somerville protests.

c) The airline pilot points out that you can't cross oceans by train. Train driver says you can already cross the English Channel, and more tunnels/bridges will follow, as in Scandinavia. Pilot says planes will always be faster. Driver points out delays getting to and from airports – and high-speed trains can take you right to the centre of cities. Driver points out good pollution figures for trains. Pilot claims damage to the troposphere is much exaggerated by the anti-flying lobby.

Additional assignment

Write to some international airlines and ask for their policy statements on the environment. Compare the various statements and try to decide how credible they are.

Mont Blanc Tunnel Inferno

Harry de Quetteville, Susannah Herbert

About the text

This dramatic account of the fire in the Mont Blanc tunnel was chosen as a very good example of what we could call the "Titanic syndrome" – the tendency of our species to assume that our technology is infallible, and not take the necessary precautions until there has been a catastrophic failure. This phenomenon is sometimes referred to as "shutting the stable door after the horse has gone".

About the photograph

The photograph shows the twisted and blackened remains of vehicles which have been gutted by the intense heat of the fire, which was fanned by wind blowing through the tunnel (apparently reinforced by the ventilation fans), until it reached the intensity of a furnace. No one caught in this inferno had a chance of survival. Even the concrete roof of the tunnel collapsed in the immediate vicinity of the fire.

Synopsis of the text

A British driver was among 35 people killed in a terrible fire in the Mont Blanc tunnel. Twenty-three lorries, nine cars and a van were gutted in the fire, which broke out in the middle of the seven-mile tunnel. Conditions for firefighters inside the tunnel were indescribable. Many victims were burned beyond recognition.
The fire started in a lorry travelling from France to Italy with a load of flour and margarine. The driver stopped and ran for his life. The following vehicles were trapped as flames and smoke spead back rapidly from the burning vehicle, fanned by a strong air current.
The fire raises a number of safety issues. The 34-year-old, heavily-used tunnel is of single-tube design, has poor ventilation and poorly-equipped emergency services. Regulations for dangerous loads do not appear to be properly enforced. The design does not compare well with more modern tunnels such as the Channel Tunnel. Witnesses claim that tunnel personnel reacted slowly to news of the fire.

Unterrichts-empfehlungen

Die Fotografie der Tunnelruine fordert die Schülerinnen und Schüler zu einer Auseinandersetzung mit der traurigen Wirklichkeit heraus, dass für viele Menschen von Verkehrs- und anderen Unglücksfällen eine große Faszination ausgeht (ARD und ZDF erzielten mit ihrer Berichterstattung über den Concorde Absturz im Juli 2000 Rekord-Einschaltquoten). Im Sinne einer kritischen Medienerziehung kann näher auf diese Thematik eingegangen werden. Dabei sollten die Schüler auch die eigene Haltung gegenüber der Sensationsberichterstattung kritisch hinterfragen.
Die genaue Beschäftigung und Analyse der Berichterstattung über das Tunnelunglück durch eine namhafte britische Zeitung (*Daily Telegraph*) kann anschließend folgen. Der erste Teil der *Activities* zielt vornehmlich auf eine Beschäftigung und Auseinandersetzung mit den Kompositionsstrategien des Zeitungsartikels ab.
Bei dieser Gelegenheit bietet es sich an, das Vorwissen der Kursteilnehmer in Bezug auf die unterschiedliche Berichterstattung der Presse zu aktivieren. Zentrale Merkmale eines „factual report" im Gegensatz zu einer „sensational news story" könnten an dieser Stelle Gewinn bringend wiederholt werden.
Die Fragen der „Unanswered questions" lassen sich gut auf verschiedene Gruppen verteilen. Dies ermöglicht den Vorteil einer recht zügigen, aber dennoch ertragreichen und umfassenden Bearbeitung. Die Lernenden sollten die Antworten auf einer Folie festhalten. Die verbleibende Arbeitsanweisung („The Titanic Syndrome") kann sinnvoll im Rahmen einer schriftlichen Hausaufgabe gelöst werden.

Assignments

Pre-reading tasks

Disasters in far-away places and close to home p. 47

Why do you think the German autobahn police say *"Kracht es rechts, kracht es gleich links"?*

Because people slowing down to have a look the accident (rubber-necking) do not keep their eyes on the road, with the result that they often have a nose to tail crash themselves.

Talk about disasters you have seen reported yourself, or which you know of from films, etc.

e.g.
- the Eschede ICE crash
- the Titanic disaster
- the Hindenburg disaster
- the Lockerbie bombing (jumbo jet crashes onto Scottish village)
- Chernobyl
- earthquakes
- tornadoes
- famines

People say that there is more interest in a child run over in the next street than in an earthquake in a remote part of the world with thousands killed. Do you agree?

Most people would agree. It is only human to be affected more by the death of someone we actually know, than of people who live thousands of miles away. However, dramatic television coverage brings disasters in other parts of the world into our living rooms nowadays, and people in Germany respond generously to appeals for help.

What brought the Mont Blanc fire "close to home" for Germans?

The facts that there were German victims and that many Germans know this tunnel, or other similar tunnels in the Alps, as part of familiar holiday routes to the south. There will have been a strong feeling that "it could have happened to us".

Activities

Different kinds of report p. 49

1. Why do you think journalists chose to wait until about half-way through the article before describing events in chronological order?

They wanted to get the drama/horror of the disaster across first before going into detail. They also wanted to mention the fact that a British driver was involved.

2. Pick out some terms which occur several times in the course of the article and comment on their use.

e.g., indescribable, fumes, black/blackened, (on) fire, oven, choking, black/blackened, flames
All these terms emphasise the catastrophic effects of a fire in a tunnel, fanned by a powerful air current.

3. Write a straightforward factual account of the disaster in about 150 words.

(See the synopsis above)

4. How might a survivor describe his experiences? Write a dramatic first-person account based on the information above.

Sample opening sentences:
We drove into the tunnel without a care in the world – we were all in a holiday mood, of course. Then we saw this cloud of black smoke ahead. At first we weren't too worried, but then we had to stop because of stationary vehicles ahead, and in no time at all fumes engulfed the car. At that moment I realised that we could die if we didn't react quickly. Other cars were stopping behind us. There was no room to turn round. We were trapped. I wrenched open the car door ...

Unanswered questions p. 49

1. Why did the driver of the burning vehicle abandon it without trying to put out the fire?

There were already flames under his cab/cabin. However, he did probably panic (naturally enough in the circumstances), and might have been able to get to his fire extinguisher (which would probably have been ineffective) or drive out of the tunnel, thus avoiding the disaster.

2. Why did the fire spread so quickly and develop such tremendous heat?

Margarine would burn fiercely, and the flames were fanned by a powerful air current in the tunnel (wind and possibly the ventilation fans).

3. Why was the earlier fire service report ignored?

We can only speculate here, but likely reasons are bureaucratic inefficiency, inertia, and unwillingness to spend large sums of money as the tunnel had not had a serious fire in the past (the Titanic syndrome – see *About the text* above).

4. Why was only one tunnel built in the first place?

To save money, of course, but possibly there was less traffic thirty odd years ago, and a more relaxed attitude to safety (refuges were not installed until 1991).

4. How could the disaster have been avoided?

In various ways, e.g.
- if there had been automatic sprinklers at intervals and/or or a very efficient firefighting service
- if the driver had managed to put out the fire or drive out of the tunnel
- if the ban on flammable loads had been properly enforced
- if there had been safe refuges or a second/third tunnel with access from the first at intervals.

Write an essay in which you discuss the facts that we human beings often seem to be too confident that things which we have built cannot fail, and ignore obvious dangers until something dreadful happens.
Refer in your answer to other disasters which have shocked the world or which, as we say, are "waiting to happen".

The *Titanic* syndrome p. 49

Individual work based on events and issues raised during work on the text. It would be worth mentioning the Victorian belief in progress, which was shattered by the Titanic disaster and the First World War, but which is always ready to reassert itself, in spite of all the evidence to the contrary. Among some disasters waiting to happen one could list, for example:
- Airports which have planes coming in low over high-density housing.
- Populations living in areas prone to flooding.
- Risks arising from the planting of genetically-modified crops.
- Holes in the ozone layer, which we may be in the process of destroying altogether (dramatic situation already in Australia, where there are serious risks of skin cancer for sunbathers).

Planners Condemn Secret Eco-Village

Simon de Bruxelles

About the text

This text is a good example of the way in which "the authorities" often put obstacles in the way of people who are trying to do something unconventional, even if the intention, as in this case, is entirely laudable.
The text deals with a "green" community which was set up in a national park without official sanction, and was condemned by the park authority for not keeping to the rules.

Synopsis of the text

A pilot saw something on a Welsh hillside which wasn't on the map, and later discovered a secret village which was almost entirely environmentally friendly and self-sufficient. As the community members had not applied for permission to build their "eco-village", the authorities intended to evict them and destroy the village. The villagers felt that the authorities did not understand what they were tyring to do, and were determined to appeal against this decision.
The twelve adults and ten children of the community had constructed a number of wooden buildings, including a roundhouse with a turf roof (see the photo), and dug a small lake. Their electric power came from solar panels, a wind generator and a water turbine. The leaders of the community were an architectural historian and his wife. They began by renovating an old farmhouse and later converted some outbuildings into a hostel for backpackers. They ran various courses in order to generate additional income.
They felt disappointed that the authorities refused to allow them to continue with their community. Support for their appeal came from the West Wales Energy Centre, but the chairman of the park committee remained adamant, in spite of sympathy for the aims of the group. He made it clear that the reason for the decision to destroy the community was that they began building without permission.

Unterrichtsempfehlungen

Als Alternative zu der *pre-reading task* „The authorities versus the ecologists" bietet es sich an, die Überschrift des Times-Artikels („Planners Condemn Secret Eco Village") an die Tafel zu schreiben. Bei geschlossenen Büchern wird den Schülerinnen und Schülern dann der Impuls gegeben, anhand der Überschrift über denkbare Aussagen des Textes zu spekulieren. Sicherlich werden in diesem Zusammenhang auch Vermutungen angestellt werden, warum von offizieller Seite das „Eco-village" abgelehnt wurde.
Im Anschluss an die Lektüre des Textes und der Sicherung des Textverständnisses kann sich einer intensiven Spracharbeit zugewandt werden, indem „lexical items" in Bezug auf das umweltfreundliche Projekt der Dorfgemeinschaft aus dem Text herausgesucht werden (Aufgabe 1). Zunächst kann diese Aufgabe in Einzelarbeit angegangen werden; die daraus hervorgehenden Ergebnisse sollten jedoch zusammengefasst in einem Tafelan-

schrieb gesichert werden. Die Aufgabe führt den Schülerinnen und Schülern exemplarisch eine sinnvolle und bewährte Lernmethode vor Augen, die sprachliche Kompetenz im Hinblick auf ein spezielles Thema zu potenzieren.
Das Abfassen eines Textes über die Dorfgemeinschaft wird den Lernenden nun sicherlich leichter von der Hand gehen.

Assignments

Pre-reading task

The authorities versus the ecologists p. 50

Read the headline and try to imagine something so environmentally friendly as an "eco-village" might be opposed by official planners.

Ideas which students might come up with:
- bureaucracy
- possibly not hygienic
- no building allowed in national parks/areas of outstanding natural beauty
- members of community not paying their local taxes

While-reading tasks

p. 51

Why do you think there is rural depopulation in Wales (and many other country areas)?

People move to the towns because it is very difficult to make a living from farming – and farming is a very hard way of life for small farmers anyway, with long hours, tiring physical work and hardly any holidays.

p. 51

Comment on the use of *even* here.

The use of *even* implies that it is in some way remarkable that there is enough electricity to power the computer, but in fact computers do not use very much electricity. So either the author is unaware of this, or he finds it surprising that this kind of community uses something as hi-tech as a computer.

p. 51

Just how "secret" is the community really?

Not very. If backpackers arrive there to stay the night and people can enrol for courses there, it is obvious that the existence of the community is known to quite a lot of people, perhaps even to the park authorities. It was probably the publicity arising from pilot's investigation which forced them to take action.

Activities

Environmentally friendly p. 52

1. Collect lexical items from the text which refer to the environmentally friendly nature of the experimental community.

e.g. self-sufficient, generating its own electricity, growing its/their own food/vegetables, using solar panels/a wind generator/a water turbine, homes of wood and turf, taking care of the land, (living) in a sustainable way, mainly vegetarian, (living) off the land, using water from a stream/lake, using wood from a copse.

2. Use them to write a paragraph in which you explain what the community is trying to do.

Sample paragraph:
The community aims to be almost entirely self-sufficient. It generates its own electricity by means of solar panels, a wind generator and a water turbine. It also grows its own vegetables for the mainly vegetarian members of the group. They try to do everything in an environmentally friendly way, building their houses from wood and turf, taking care of the land, using water from a stream and burning wood from a copse which will soon be replaced by new growth.

The other side of the case p. 52

Write – and practise with a partner – an argument in which a planner tries to convince a member of the community that their eco-village should not have been built.

Suggested start:
Planner: Good morning, Mr Orbach. We are very sorry that your buildings are going to have to be destroyed.
Orbach: What do you mean, *have to* be destroyed. You only want to demolish them because of stupid regulations.
Planner: We don't agree that the regulations are stupid. They are merely intended to protect the natural environment in the park.
Orbach: But that's exactly what ***we*** are trying to do!
Planner: That may be true, but you should have applied for permission first.
Orbach: Well, to be honest, the community just sort of developed. There was no one time when we felt, "Hey, we'd better ask the park authority if this is OK."
Planner: Well it isn't OK, and it's all going to have to come down!
Orbach: Give me one good reason for wrecking our work.
Planner: ...

Realistic or utopian? p. 52

In some ways this community sounds like the sort of place where many people would like to live. How about you? Write an essay in which you weigh up the arguments for and against this way of life.

Arguments for:
- low impact on the environment
- healthy way of life
- nice country area
- physical work to do – easy to keep fit
- sense of community
- self-sufficiency
- no dangerous chemicals in food

Arguments against:
- probably boring for city-dwellers – lack of entertainment
- small, enclosed community

- need to run courses etc. to make a living
- would not survive a bad drought/a really hard winter
- way of life a bit primitive in some ways
- no mention of education for the children
- not attractive for non-gardeners/farmers
- not really self-sufficient – would have to buy most of their equipment, for example (solar sells, wind generator etc.)

Additional assignment

Do you know of any cases of bureaucratic resistance to environmentally friendly measures in your area? You could talk to journalists at the local newspaper offices if you don't know of any cases at first hand. Some typical examples would be:

- Resisting the introduction of wind generators
- Not letting people use "grey" water for flushing toilets
- The authorities often insist on houses being connected to mains water and drains, even if people have made satisfactory arrangements of their own
- Killing wild plants on verges and in hedgerows
- Destroying the habitats of rare plants/animals by building houses/roads/out of town shopping centres/malls.
- Various forms of discrimination against "bio" (organic) farmers

It would be wrong to assume that the "green" point of view is always right. Discuss the cases you find with your fellow-students and try to decide where you stand.

Boom or Doom? Stephen Speight

About the text

This fictionalised dialogue is intended to bring home to readers that there is no simple solution to environmental and other problems of our immensely complex world. It also demonstrates that people from similar backgrounds can disagree fundamentally on basic issues. It is hoped that the language chosen can serve as a model for reasonably polite discussions between students on topics similar to those covered in the textbook.

Synopsis of the text

Old schoolfriends John and Naomi meet again by chance after many years. After the usual polite exchanges they immediately start to disagree with one another as they did in the past, because of their fundamentally different outlooks and careers. John works for the oil industry, and Naomi is a "green" politician. Her claim that the oil industry is bad for the environment is countered by John's statement about the huge sums which the oil industry spends on avoiding pollution. They go on to disagree about the dangers caused by more and more traffic on the roads, and what the consequences would be if people in Asia started driving large numbers of cars. John claims that we need not worry about the oil running out, and says that the Indians and Chinese should put

their own houses in order by means of birth control. This makes Naomi angry. She points out that the Chinese already exercise strict birth control, and that Indians consume far less energy per head of population than we do. John is able to score a point because Naomi herself goes to work by car, at least in winter. He follows this up by saying that a low-tech approach would put millions of people out of work in the industrialised countries. We did not run out of coal, and we will have moved on to other sources of energy before the oil runs out. Naomi hopes he is not referring to nuclear power, and says that we are using up all kinds of resources very fast, and killing off all kinds of rare species in the process. John agrees that this is bad, but says poor people need to eat, and they can't live off the rain forests.
Naomi feels that our species is the problem, but John points out that only human beings create art and music. We have quite a lot to be proud of in spite of all the terrible things we are responsible for. His view of the future is fairly optimistic, but Naomi thinks our planet is probably doomed.

About the graph

The graph was chosen as a particularly striking view of population growth from prehistoric times up to today, with present growth rates projected into the not very distant future. Very slow growth rates in the past have become explosive over the past century or so, with consequences which no one can reliably predict, but which are likely to be catastrophic unless ways are found of reversing the trend. It should be pointed out to students that growth rates in industrial countries are low, even negative in some cases. Really rapid growth is in parts of the world which have all kinds of problems to deal with even without more and more mouths to feed every year.

Unterrichtsempfehlungen

Im Rahmen der *Activities* zu den vorangegangenen Texten haben die Schülerinnen und Schüler schon einige dialogische Texte verfasst. „Boom or Doom?“ ermöglicht es den Kursteilnehmern nun, sich bewusst mit einem Dialog auseinander zu setzen, welcher von einem Muttersprachler produziert wurde. Im Zusammenhang mit der Erschließungsarbeit wird es sich als ertragreich erweisen, das Augenmerk der Schülerinnen und Schüler auf die Art der Gesprächsführung, aber auch auf für Gespräche typische Redemittel zu lenken. Die erste *while-reading task* bietet diesbezüglich eine sehr gute Anknüpfungsmöglichkeit.
Der Aufgabenapparat zielt vorrangig auf eine Beschäftigung mit den Vor- und Nachteilen des Erdöls für unsere moderne Welt ab („The arguments“ / „Oil-friend or enemy?“). Vor dem Hintergrund dieser Problematik besteht die Möglichkeit, eine angeregte Podiumsdiskussion in Gang zu bringen.

Assignments

While-reading tasks

What conversational functions does this first section fulfil? p. 52

- greeting
- small talk
- exchange of compliments
- establishing a basis for discussion

Why do you think we still use so much petrol and diesel when cars really are more efficient than they were in the past? p. 52

- Modern cars have a lot of safety and luxury equipment which makes them heavy.
- People travel longer distances more frequently than they used to (miles or kilometres per year), particularly owners of larger, thirstier cars.
- Sales of cars have increased, and proportionately more people drive large, high-performance cars.
- Performance has improved across the board. We use the improved performance, which cancels out the improved economy.

What do you think of this argument? p. 53

It is very short-sighted, and it is arrogant of people in the industrial nations to tell other parts of the world what we think would be good for them (meaning good for us, of course).

Which is worse? A small family and high energy consumption, or a large family and low energy consumption? p. 53

This is not easy to answer. There is no doubt that the industrial nations use far more than their fair share of energy, but on the other hand they also produce more goods and have achieved a high standard of living for their citizens. A large family in a developing country may not consume much energy, but its members are likely to be poor, badly-nourished and housed, and without much education. Some would say it is possible to be just as happy without much in the way of material goods, but given the choice, most people would choose wealth. However, rich nations employ a lot more psychiatrists!

What do you think the answer is? p. 53

Naomi almost certainly drives to work in the winter.

Whose pockets do you think the money would probably end up in? p. 54

Much of the money would find its way into the pockets of corrupt politicians and businessmen.

What is rather surprising about this speech of John's? p. 54

Up until now he has not seemed to be the sort of person who would appreciate the arts, but it is of course possible to be an oilman (or work for a tobacco company, etc.) and cultured at the same time. This is one of the many paradoxes of our species.

p. 54 ➤

What is wrong with monocultures?

- One species of plant means a limited range of wild life.
- Greater risk of attack by pests or disease.
- Unnatural, less attractive than the wonderful variety which nature produces when left to itself.

Activities

The arguments ➤ p. 55

1. This discussion is a bit like a boxing match. List the arguments put forward by each speaker and the answer given by his/her opponent.

Naomi: Oil industry bad for the environment
John: Spends billions on avoiding pollution.
John: Cars clean and economical nowadays.
Naomi: The air is still more polluted (more cars on the road)
Naomi: Pleased that oil shortages will eventually stop pollution.
John: All kinds of useful products made from oil.
Oil will not run out anyway.
Naomi: Whose argument is this (implies that this is the oil companies' view)? Will not be true if Chinese and Indians buy cars.
John: Oil will not run out in the near future. Birth control needed in India and China.
Naomi: China already has strict birth control. Indians use very little in the way of resources. We use huge quantities of energy.
John: Naomi probably uses nearly as much energy as he does.
Naomi: Rides a cycle to work.
John: But not in the winter. Then she drives her car to work.
John: Low-tech approach would cause unemployment and reduce our standard of living.
Naomi: But we would be living in a cleaner world with sustainable use of resources.
John: We will move on to new resources before we run out.
Naomi: Dangerous nuclear power?
John: Nuclear power stations do not produce greenhouse gases.
Naomi: Radiation sickness and cancers instead.
John: Modern nuclear power stations are safe.
Naomi: We are wrecking our world by using up resources and killing off thirty species a day.
John: Poor people can't afford to worry about the environment.
Naomi: We should be prepared to pay them to do so.
John: The money would go to the wrong people.
Naomi: Our species is the problem.
John: But only we humans are capable of appreciating our world.
Naomi: We won't be around for much longer.
John: We will solve our problems and survive. We will learn to manage our resources as with the Swedish forests.
Naomi: Monocultures are not satisfactory.

2. Which speaker do you think has the stronger case? Give reasons for your decision.

Most students will probably choose the environmentalist case, but for rather naive reasons. In fact, the true price of most commodities (e.g. copper) has fallen in recent years and will probably continue to do so because we are so good at finding better substitutes. However, oil is consumed in such vast quantities that it may really become scarce before there are viable alternatives. The ideal would of course be low energy hi-tech with a caring, human face. The computer/internet/mobile phone revolution is not particularly energy-hungry, and may in the long run mean that people travel less, use less trees for making paper, etc. But the appetite for travel is unlikely to diminish – unless people from the industrialised nations become afraid to travel far afield in case they are taken hostage or become the victims of other, worse crimes.

Oil – friend or enemy? p. 55

To a very large extent our world runs on oil. Write a paragraph in which you discuss the benefits and disadvantages which this state of affairs has brought to the world.

Points which could be made:
Benefits:
- mobility for nearly everyone
- oil is still fairly cheap
- easily transported
- high energy content
- cleaner than coal
- possible to design clean-burning engines and heating systems

Disadvantages:
- causes air pollution
- oil spills at sea contaminate beaches, destroy wild life
- oil prices can be manipulated by various groups (OPEC, oil companies)
- fossil fuel, irreplaceable, supplies are finite
- better to use oil for producing plastics and medicines than burning it

The great paradox p. 55

Write an essay in which you discuss the inability of science to deal with what we might call the human factor.

Some thoughts to help students get started:
- Clever scientists can solve most scientific and technical problems, given enough time and money.
- This money is not always wisely spent – sometimes huge sums are wasted on projects which come to nothing.
- We are less successful at dealing with diseases such as cancer and AIDS, although progress is being made.
- As a species we are not very good at thinking logically – less worried by invisible threats to our health and the environment than we should be.
- We are also less worried than we should be when we open “Pandora’s Box” e.g. when we enter new areas of research such as genetic engineering without any reliable knowledge of the consequences.

- We appear to be very ineffective when it comes to solving problems arising from poverty, over-population, unemployment, etc. There are persistent pockets of poverty even in rich countries.
- We are very easily led astray by charismatic dictators, demagogues, sect leaders, etc., sometimes with truly disastrous consequences.
- It is quite possible that our species is genetically programmed to fight – this may be how the "fittest" survive.

About the final photograph

The photograph shows a typical confrontation between a tourist from an industrial nation and members of the indigent (probably African) population. The tourist is fat, and dressed unflatteringly in "Hawaii-type" shorts, shirt and sunhat, while the woman is slender, as is her son, and elegantly/tastefully dressed in flowing robes and some kind of headscarf. Her crouched pose suggests humility. She is selling pineapple-like fruits to the tourist, using sign language to tell him the price. The photographer has chosen to set up the scene against a background of sand, ocean and distant palm trees, with no other people in sight. The viewpoint is low, which adds to the rather stark impression.
Most "Westerners" will find the photograph embarrassing to contemplate, for reasons which students might like to speculate on. They should also try to imagine how the woman feels. The economics of the scene are worth discussing, too.

Additional texts

Flights of Fancy Fred Guterl

On July 26, 2000, a Concorde crashed immediately after takeoff, killing everyone on board and a few people in the nearly empty hotel which it hit. Dramatic photographs taken by an amateur photographer at the scene brought home the full horror of the disaster to everyone. The plane was already in the air, but failing to gain height, and a huge plume of flame could be seen at the rear. The people on board had only a few more seconds to live.
The cause of the accident was probably a piece of metal on the runway which destroyed the tyre of the nosewheel, parts of which ruptured fuel tanks and damaged hydraulic systems. This made it impossible for the pilots to control the plane. On the Concorde, the delta design means that tanks and control systems are vulnerable to this kind of damage. Althought there had never been a Concorde crash before, there had been various potentially dangerous "incidents" in the past, arising mainly from this feature of the design. The plane's safety record was not a good as it seemed. At the time of writing (September 2000), all Concordes were grounded, and their future was uncertain.

When an icon of technological achievement goes down in flames, it is hard not to wonder what will happen next. Does the crash of Air France 4590 signify the end of supersonic-plane travel, just as the

Hindenburg disaster spelled the end of dirigibles? Will succeeding generations know the Concorde as the first and last supersonic transport?

There's no way of knowing, but this much is certain: legions of engineers around the world have been attacking the myriad problems associated with supersonic travel ever since the Concordes first began rumbling down runways in the 1960s. They are at it still. Japan is testing models. Entrepreneurs are hatching business jets, France is contemplating its own supersonic program and researchers are dreaming up planes that fly as fast as rockets. Listening to them, it's almost possible to believe that faster-than-sound travel might one day be the norm, rather than merely a specialty for the fashionable rich.

To be sure, supersonic transports, or SSTs, are terrifically difficult to pull off. Passengers will pay only a modest premium for the privilege of flying in them. Because SSTs trail shock waves, which account for the notorious sonic boom, they are restricted to a narrow market of overseas flights. And SSTs get no exemption from ever more stringent airport noise and environmental regulations.

Any new commercially viable SST would have to best the Concorde by a long shot. It would have to carry two or three times the Concorde's 100-or-so passengers. It would have to cross the Pacific Ocean without refueling, which calls for an innovative new airframe that cuts supersonic drag to an absolute minimum. And those noise restrictions mean requiring it to take off and land using less thrust than the noisy Concorde. It's enough to drive an aerodynamicist crazy. Engineers recite a litany of such conflicting requirements, which push development costs sky-high – to $30 billion by some estimates. That's a lot of money to bet on a project that sits outside the mainstream. The leading edge of plane design is the superjumbo Airbus A3XX, built to ferry the most passengers at the least cost per head.

Yet the lure of supersonic travel remains strong. In March 2002, Japan's National Aeronautics Laboratory plans to test a one-tenth-scale model of a supersonic transport, NEXST 1. It will ride piggyback on a rocket to an altitude of 17 kilometers, separate from the booster and glide earthward, testing how well its sleek shape reduces drag. In 2005, a NEXST 2 is slated to fly with its own engines. By 2015 Japan hopes to build an SST capable of carrying 250 passengers from Tokyo to Los Angeles in four hours.

Can Japan's aerospace industry pull it off? NASA engineers think so. They were developing a plane the size and range of Japan's but 25 percent faster – designed to fly at 2.5 times the speed of sound. Their design was twice as efficient as the Concorde at subsonic speeds. But tighter noise restrictions were announced at a critical juncture in the program, forcing NASA back to the drawing board and giving airplane makers cold feet.

William Gilbert, a technical manager on the NASA program, believes that the technology favors a slightly slower, but still supersonic, plane – such as Japan's. "We wanted to do 12-hour flights in four hours," he says. "But if you bring the speed down a bit, you still have a very fast plane, and you get a lot more leeway in the design."

This lesson is not lost on Japan's NAL. Its nine-year, 28 billion-yen program is testing whether a plane could be built to fly no faster than the Concorde – just better. "The Concorde is small and noisy and less than efficient," says Dr. Kimio Sakata, head of NAL's Advanced Technology Aircraft Project Center. "Our new aircraft must be commercially viable and environmentally friendly."

Supersonic Milestones
Among many failed attempts to build a supersonic jet over the years, only the Concorde made it.
1962 France and Britain sign a treaty to jointly develop the Concorde
1965 The Soviet Union unveils the design of its Tu-144 supersonic transport (SST), dubbed "Concordski"
1966 The Federal Aviation Commission selects Boeing to build an SST
1968 First Concorde
1971 The U.S. cancels its SST project
1973 The Tu-144 crashes near Paris; eventually the U.S.S.R. abandons the project
1976 The Concorde makes its first commercial passenger flights
1997 Japan begins developing scale models of a next-generation SST
1999 U.S. manufacturers pull out of a NASA SST development project
2000 A Concorde crashes outside Paris, killing all aboard

None of Us Lives In a Vacuum John Browne

The oil and gas industry is in the middle of a revolution, one taking place on five or six different fronts. After 70 years with an almost unchanged corporate structure among the major companies, the industry has, in the last two years, seen four major transactions in the United States and Europe, and a host of smaller linkups. Companies have grown in scope and scale. But oil prices are still largely determined by the decisions of OPEC; when all the mergers are completed, the four largest companies together will account for no more than 12 percent of world oil supply and 13 percent of gas supplies.
These mergers and acquisitions don't constitute an endgame; the industry is not shrinking. Demand for oil is 12 percent higher than it was a decade ago. Gas demand is 30 percent higher. And with nuclear developments again in question it seems certain that hydrocarbons will meet the bulk of the world's new energy demand for the foreseeable future. The geography of the industry is changing, too. Incremental demand for energy comes predominantly from Asia, driven by population growth and rising living standards.
We are seeing a new balance of fuels take shape. The demand for natural gas has doubled since the early 1970s and is set to double again by 2020, partly because gas is more environmentally friendly – for equivalent electricity output, gas generates less than half the emissions produced by coal. As part of China's celebrations of the 50th anniversary of the revolution, the Chinese adjusted the use of some of the coal-fired industrial plants around Beijing. In a city that is often covered by a blanket of smog, people could see what they were celebrating.

That story is just one example of a new set of expectations. People want energy, because energy means liberty, mobility, growth and the chance to improve living standards. But people want a clean environment, too. Yet at the moment consumers and government seem to be in denial. They refuse to accept their own responsibility for increasing costs to the quality of life which are imposed when we all demand more. And they deflect that responsibility onto the oil and gas sector. There are no simple and easy answers to global warming, traffic congestion, air quality and waste disposal. Oil companies can't solve these problems on their own. But we can make a contribution as part of a common effort. We all need to take measures that transcend the apparent – and unacceptable – trade-off between better living standards and pollution.

Take climate change. I disagree with those in our industry who believe that the only answer to climate change and global warming is to question the science, deny responsibility and ignore reality. Of course, the science is provisional; there are many things we do not know. But it is an undeniable truth that people link energy to pollution, that they fear for the environmental future and that they believe companies should raise their aspirations. We did some polling; when asked whether they associate energy with progress or pollution, almost 40 percent of respondents say the first association is with pollution. But 80 percent believe that business has the ability and the responsibility to find answers.

We can't afford to disappoint them. That's why, in a speech at Yale last year, I committed BP to reducing our own emissions of greenhouse gases by at least 10 percent from a 1990 base by the year 2010. Because our business is growing rapidly, that is a reduction of more than 40 percent from the level we would have reached if we took no action at all. And it's why we've pledged this year to introduce new clean fuels in at least 40 cities around the world by the end of the year 2000.

But our decisions on global warming and clean fuels also taught us a larger truth. We learned that for a company like ours – indeed, for any international company with a large number of highly skilled employees – top management can no longer expect to make policy in a vacuum. When we accepted that, on the evidence, global warming was a true problem, we did so in part because many of our own employees had told us that we couldn't go on living in denial. Their families, and their children in particular, believed we were *part* of that problem. Our staff found it intolerable that we seemed to be on the wrong side of a fundamental issue. I have never received so many personal e-mails from BP Amoco employees as I did after announcing our new policy. A few weeks later we asked all our teams for their direct support, so that we could identify ways of reducing our own emissions. I got hundreds of pages of e-mail from people all around the world with detailed practical suggestions.

The old order, symbolized by the remote and arrogant corporation, convinced of its own virtue and invincibility, is passing. The new order is neither comfortable nor predictable; but it reminds us that companies, however big, are simply servants of society. We exist only because someone wants to buy what we provide. In a complex world, the companies that thrive will be those that can combine the traditional strengths, like a strong financial balance sheet and a great portfolio of assets, with something new: the capacity to listen and to learn.

JOHN BROWNE *is the chief executive officer of BP Amoco.*

Teil III

Klausurbeispiele

Klausur 1

Brave New World Signalled by 300mph Levitating Trains in Airport Link-up

Robin McKie

Passengers could soon be hurtled at more than 300 mph on levitating trains that run through vacuum tunnels hundreds of feet underground. Services would link major airports, such as Heathrow and Gatwick, cutting transfer times to a few minutes, say engineers.

In the longer term, a network of high-speed, metro trains could be constructed across Europe, they add.

The system has been dubbed the Underground Concorde and is the brainchild of a European consortium backed by Daimler-Chrysler, Alstrom and several major civil engineering companies.

The Swiss Government has asked the group to design a £3 billion, 55-mile underground line that could whisk passengers between Zurich and Basle airports in less than 10 minutes. It is also hoped that Geneva and Lyons airports could be similarly connected.

'Our train technology could transform the airports of tomorrow,' said Dr Michele Mossi, a director of the consortium, Swissmetro.

'By providing near instantaneous transfers between terminals in different cities, we will be creating new, super-airports from flight centres dozen of miles apart.'

The new system is based on magnetic levitation. Instead of running on wheels, carriages and engines would float, suspended by powerful magnetic fields, while linear induction motors would propel trains through their tunnel.

'This suspension technology has been proven in trials in Germany and Japan,' added Mossi. 'However, we have added a new twist. We will run levitation trains through tunnels from which we have pumped nearly all the air. This will greatly reduce atmospheric resistance and allow us to operate even faster, and more efficient trains.'

Under the consortium plans, air pressure in metro tunnels would be reduced to a fraction of their normal levels – to the equivalent of the atmosphere 55,000ft above sea level, the cruising altitude of Concorde. 'Essentially, we are going to build supersonic planes that will fly underground,' he said.

Apart from boosting train speeds, depressurised tunnels will allow designers to construct extremely compact trains. Each carriage would be less than 10ft in diameter, while tunnels would be only 16ft across. Such restricted dimensions should help to make significant reductions in construction costs.

However, to prevent passengers collapsing from lack of air as they enter or leave trains, airlocks will have to be constructed at each station.

It is expected that trains carrying 200 passengers would run every four minutes once the system is fully operational.

'We originally planned to build a £62bn pilot link between Lausanne and Geneva, but have been told by the Swiss government that revenue from such a line would not be sufficient to justify the investment,' Mossi added.

'Instead officials have asked us to draw up proposals for a more expensive pilot line – between Zurich and Basle airports. The line would be 90 kilometres (about 55 miles) long and trains running at 500 kilometres an hour [about 300mph] would be able to do the journey in about 10 minutes.'

The project is to be discussed by project leaders, as well as officials from Zurich and Basle local authorities and also Swiss airport delegates this week.

It is expected most concerns about the system will focus on its cost. With its £3bn price tag, and as yet untested vacuum technology, the Zurich-Basle Underground Concorde requires a significant capital outlay.

This point is acknowledged by the consortium, though its engineers point out that its costs are comparable with those of the latest generation European TGV train lines on the surface. They say the latter cost about £25 million a mile to build, while their new levitation train line would eventually cost about £38m a mile to construct – underground where they cause no noise or pollution.

Other problems to be overcome will include those concerned with heat buildup in the tunnels, which may have to be cooled to prevent outbreaks of fire.

The consortium has already begun work on a scaled-down line half-a-kilometre long near Lausanne, and will begin trials there in a few months. If approved by the Swiss parliament in June, work on the full-scale pilot line between Zurich and Basle would begin in 2002, but it will take take several years to complete.

Assignments

1. Briefly describe how the new levitating trains are supposed to work and what main function they would serve.
2. What major problems and concerns have to be overcome to realize the project?
3. Analyse ll. 1–45 and explain their effect on the reader.
4. Have a careful look at the headline. What could it reveal about the author's attitude towards the new levitating trains?
5. It is your choice now. Please select one of the following items:
   a) Imagine you are one of the first passengers on the new train from Zurich to Basle. After your arrival in Basle you <u>write a letter</u> to your girlfriend/boyfriend about your
      - feelings
      - thoughts
      - impressions and
      - conversations with other passengers during the trip.
   b) Imagine you are one of the first passengers on the train from Zurich to Basle. After your arrival in Basle you are interviewed by a reporter from a famous newspaper (The

Times ... The Independent ...). Write an interview in which the reporter asks you about your
- feelings
- thoughts
- impressions and
- conversations with other passengers during the trip.

6. Do you personally think that we need these new high-speed, levitating trains? Give reasons.

Solutions

1. The levitating trains would be suspended just above the track by powerful magnetic fields. The equipment in the train which creates this field, and the track itself, together form linear motors which would drive/propel the train at very high speeds. The new feature of this system compared with the German *Transrapid* is that the trains would travel in vacuum tunnels/tunnels from which nearly all the air has been pumped. This would greatly reduce atmospheric resistance/friction. The main function of these trains in the near future would be to link major airports. Later there could be a high-speed underground rail network across Europe.

2. Major problems and concerns:
   - As there would be hardly any air in the tunnels, airlocks would have to be constructed at each station.
   - It is possible that the trains would not make a profit because not enough passengers would use the service.
   - Costs would be extremely high (but not much higher than for the latest TGV lines).
   - Heat will build up in the tunnels, and ways must be found to cool them/prevent fires.
   - (Although the article does not specifically mention passenger safety, students may well want to mention the need for refuges, an escape tunnel etc., – the facilities which were missing or proved inadequate in the Mont Blanc tunnel disaster (see pp. 47–9 in the Students' Book).

3. The first 45 lines of the article present an entirely positive view of the planned underground rail links. The vocabulary is exaggerated to suggest tremendous speed and efficiency (e.g. *300mph levitating trains, hurtled, cutting transfer times to a few minutes, Underground Concorde, whisk, near instantaneous).* Other terms suggest drastic, revolutionary change (e.g. *hundreds of feet underground, brainchild, across Europe, transform the airports of tomorrow, new super-airports).* The effect on the reader is likely to be that he or she imagines a science-fiction-line scenario, with people flying the longer distances, going down in high-tech lifts to the trains, through the airlocks, and then being whisked off along the vacuum tunnels in levitating trains. The mention of respected engineering companies suggests to the reader that this vision could easily become reality.

4. The reference to a "brave new world" echoes the title of Huxley's famous utopian novel (see pp. 20–23 in the Student's Book). Although Huxley was almost certainly using the words ironically, the author of the article seems to believe that this new transport

system really would help to create a better world by means of technology. There is no trace of irony in the headline.

5. a) Some ideas:
feelings: excitement, apprehension, possible claustrophobia in the narrow train/airlocks/tunnel
thoughts: wonder if the technology has been tested adequately, thoughts about other train and tunnel disasters, glad when the journey is safely over, admiration for the technology itself which makes such a fast journey possible
impressions: sense of speed, slight disappointment because there is nothing to see during the journey, as in the Channel Tunnel. Feeling that it would be difficult to get out if anything went wrong.
conversations: Likely topics: Is this your first trip? Convenience of the new link, inefficiency/delays/missed flights as a result of previous inefficient airport links. Environmental issues.

Possible start:
Dearest/Darling XXX,
I have just arrived safely in Basle after a fantastic trip. As you know, I landed in Zurich, and then caught the new underground link to Basle. The trip on the new underground train was fantastic. We went down in a very fast lift, and then there was an airlock before we could get on the train. They need this airlock because ... I began to feel ... However, ...
b) Ideas as for 5a) but expressed in interview form. Possible start.
Reporter: Good morning sir/madam. I believe you have just come up from the new underground airport link. Is that correct.
Passenger: Yes, that's right. It was quite an experience.
Reporter: Tell us about your feelings,
Passenger: Well, I was a bit apprehensive, naturally ...
Reporter: Why was that?

6. **Reasons for:**
- journeys from airport to airport or from airports into cities are often slow/inconvenient
- the advantages of fast air travel are often almost cancelled out by getting to and from the airport on the ground
- no environmental impact
- if the network were to be extended across Europe, short-hop air travel would become a thing of the past
- this may be the way we will travel in the future. The sooner we start building levitating trains the better.

Reasons against:
- very expensive
- not enough people would use the service
- need for airlocks
- dangers of heat building up/fires
- safety problems of various kinds – fires, suffocation, no escape route

Klausur 2

No Swallows in Utopia H. G. Wells

He began with the fact and reverted to the fact that there were no swallows to be seen in Utopia, and there were no swallows to be seen in Utopia because there were no gnats nor midges. There had been an enormous deliberate reduction of insect life in Utopia, and that had seriously affected every sort of creature that was directly or indirectly dependent upon insect life. So soon as the new state of affairs was securely established in Utopia and the educational state working, the attention of the Utopian community had been given to the long-cherished idea of a systematic extermination of tiresome and mischievous species. A careful inquiry was made into the harmfulness and the possibility of eliminating the house-fly for example, wasps and hornets, various species of mice and rats, rabbits, stinging-nettles. Ten thousand species, from disease-germ to rhinoceros and hyena, were put upon their trial. Every species found was given an advocate. Of each it was asked: What good is it? What harm does it do? How can it be extirpated? What else may go with it if it goes? Is it worth while wiping it out of existence? Or can it be mitigated and retained? And even when the verdict was death final and complete, Utopia set about the business of extermination with great caution. A reserve would be kept and was in many cases still being kept, in some secure isolation, of every species condemned.

Most infectious and contagious fevers had been completely stamped out; some had gone very easily; some had only been driven out of human life by proclaiming a war and subjecting the whole population to discipline. Many internal and external parasites of man and animals had also been got rid of completely. And further, there had been a great cleansing of the world from noxious insects, from weeds and vermin and hostile beasts. The mosquito had gone, the house-fly, the blow-fly, and indeed a great multitude of flies had gone; they had been driven out of life by campaigns involving an immense effort and extending over many generations. It had been infinitely more easy to get rid of such big annoyances as the hyena and the wolf than to abolish these smaller pests. The attack upon the flies had involved the virtual rebuilding of a large proportion of Utopian houses and a minute cleansing of them all throughout the planet.

The question of what else would go if a certain species went was one of the most subtle that Utopia had to face. Certain insects, for example, were destructive and offensive grubs in the opening stage of their lives, were evil as caterpillar or pupa and then became either beautiful in themselves or necessary to the fertilization of some useful or exquisite flowers. Others offensive in themselves were a necessary irreplaceable food to pleasant and desirable creatures. It was not true that swallows had gone from Utopia, but they had become extremely rare; and rare too were a number of little insectivorous birds, the fly-catcher for example, that harlequin of the air. But they had not died out altogether; the extermination of insects had not gone to that length; sufficient species had remained to make some districts still habitable for these delightful birds.

Assignments

1. How is the extermination of "tiresome and mischievous species" carried out and what consequences does it have?
2. Examine ll. 7–45. How does the use of language reflect the Utopians' view about certain creatures?
3. Please choose one of the following tasks:
   a. You have been sent to Utopia to investigate Utopian life. Back at home you have to write a report about your findings and experiences in Utopia. What would you write?
   b. The Utopian community has put dogs on trial. You are their advocate. Write a report in which you argue whether dogs belong to the category of "tiresome and mischievous species" or not.
4. Can you draw any parallels between Utopia and the modern world around you? Illustrate your answer with examples.
5. Would you like to live in Utopia? Give reasons which support your point of view.

Solutions

1. Each species was put on trial to see what harm or good it did, whether other species would be affected, and whether it would be worth the effort of wiping it out. Great care was taken to weigh up all the possible consequences. Some species were easy to destroy. Others, particularly some insects, required long, difficult campaigns and far-reaching measures in order to get rid of them. Samples of most species were kept in reserve in case it became necessary to re-introduce them for some reason. The consequence of wiping out a number of species was that the world had been freed from most infectious diseases, pests, and parasites. However, some desirable species, such as swallows, had become extremely rare because most of the insects which formed their diet no longer existed.
2. The language used in lines 7–45 shows that the utopians had the following views about certain creatures:
   a) They were quite certain that it would be a good idea to exterminate certain species (e.g. *the long-cherished idea, tiresome and mischievous species).*
   b) They felt they had a perfect right to pursue this policy, and had no religious or scientific scruples about what they were doing (e.g. *systematic extermination).*
   c) They knew in advance which species they would like to destroy, and referred to them in negative terms, (e.g. *tiresome and mischievous species, infectious, contagious, parasites, noxious insects, weeds, vermin, pests).*
   d) Their policies were extremely drastic (e.g. *extermination, eliminating, wiping it out of existence, death final and complete, proclaiming a war, virtual rebuilding of a large proportion of Utopian houses).*
   e) They nevertheless took great care that mistakes were not made, and what we now call the gene pool would not lose the genetic material in those species which were destroyed *(a careful*

enquiry, every species found was given an advocate, a reserve was kept).

3. **a) Start and guidelines:**
The first thing I noticed was that there appeared to be no swallows in Utopia. I made enquiries about this, and discovered that there was a policy to abolish all "tiresome and mischievous species". I was worried that they could easily destroy the balance of nature, but was assured that extreme care was taken over the decision whether or not to exterminate a particular species.
   - the trial procedure
   - examples of species which had been exterminated
   - the reserve of condemned species
   - controversial cases
   - results of the Utopian policy
   - the fate of swallows and other insectivorous birds

   b) Arguments in favour of dogs:
   - friendly creatures
   - provide playmates for children
   - provide company for old people
   - can be trained to behave well
   - can act as guard dogs and guide dogs for the blind
   - have been domestic pets for thousands of years

   Arguments against dogs:
   - annoy people by barking, jumping up at them, etc.
   - can transmit diseases/fleas to humans
   - some dogs are dangerous (pit bulls, Rottweilers, Stafford Terriers)
   - pollute our streets and parks with excrement
   - expensive to feed, bills for injections, etc.
   - problems when the owners go on holiday

4. We can see that our world has begun to develop along the lines described in H.G. Wells' utopian novel, e.g.
   - We also try, sometimes successfully, to wipe out infectious deseases (e.g. smallpox, leprosy), either by destroying the environment in which the germs flourish, or by finding effective vaccines.
   - We are well on the way to excluding vermin and parasites (rats, mice, fleas, lice) from our houses and/or bodies, but in any kind of crisis (war, a dustmen's strike) they are always likely to return in force.
   - We are in the process of destroying large numbers of species. However, unlike the Utopians, we are doing this in a largely accidental and uncontrolled kind of way by the use of pesticides and other chemicals, and by destroying habitats.
   - We understand the need to preserve the genes of vanishing species (rare creatures kept alive in zoos or bred in captivity then returned to the wild), but we may be fighting a losing battle. Although the term had not yet been invented, Wells is talking about genetic engineering, and we do this, too.

5. **Reasons in favour of living in this Utopia:**
   - a very clean, hygienic world
   - little risk of being bitten or stung, or of catching an infectious disease
   - people would probably have long, healthy lives
   - great care taken over any decision to wipe out a species
   - a world designed to be the ideal environment for human beings

   Reasons against:
   - a world in which man has no qualms about "playing God" in various ways
   - impossible to know all the possible consequences of interfering with the balance of nature in advance, disasters quite likely
   - many people like our varied, "messy" world more or less as it is
   - if life was so easy, people might become lazy and degenerate
   - not as exciting as our world. Nothing is left to chance, no random elements

Acknowledgements

Texts

Brad Stone: "Bitten by Love" from *Newsweek,* May 15, 2000, pp. 52–53

Michael Crichton: "Cloning Dinosaurs" from *Jurassic Park* by Michael Crichton, London, Arrow Books, 1991, pp. 66-68

Isaac Asimov: "The Bicentennial Man" from *The Bicentennial Man and Other Stories* by Isaac Asimov, London, Millenium, 2000, pp. 135–136

Fred Guterl: "Flights of Fancy" from *Newsweek,* August 7, 2000, pp. 26–27

Sir John Browne: "None of us Lives in a Vacuum" from *Newsweek Special Edition,* December 1999–February 2000, p. 78

Robin McKie: "Brave New World Signalled by 300 mph Levitating Trains in Airport Link-up" from *The Observer,* April 30, 2000

H.G. Wells: "No Swallows in Utopia" from *Men Like Gods* by H.G. Wells, New York, Macmillan, 1923, pp. 84–86